The
Psychic Power
of
Children

The
Psychic Power
of
Children

Cassandra Eason

GUILD PUBLISHING
LONDON · NEW YORK · SYDNEY · TORONTO

Copyright © Cassandra Eason, 1990

This edition published 1990 by Guild Publishing
by arrangement with Rider
An imprint of Random Century Publishing Group Ltd
20 Vauxhall Bridge Road
London SW1V 2SA

Cassandra Eason's right to be identified as the author
of this work has been asserted by her in accordance
with the Copyright, Designs and Patents Act, 1988.

Set in Linotronic Baskerville by SX Composing Ltd,
Rayleigh, Essex

Printed and bound in Great Britain by Mackays of Chatham

CN 9970

Contents

1

News from Nowhere

I was in no condition to appreciate Jack's message of doom at 9 o'clock on a Sunday morning. It had been a long night. My husband John, a journalist, had been working overnight at the breakfast telelvision station TV-am, 40 miles away in London. I had been on the night shift as well with four children, the youngest, Miranda, only a few months old and teething with a vengeance.

If my two-and-a-half-year old son, Jack, had told me the world was coming to an end I would have replied: 'That's nice, but don't talk while you're eating.'

'Daddy's gone poly-boys on his motor bike, but he's all right,' said Jack calmly and carried on with his breakfast. Poly-boys was the playful expression I used when I rolled Jack on the floor while dressing him.

'That's nice,' I replied. All I could think about was that John would soon be home and there was only another 30 minutes to survive. But john was not going to be home in 30 minutes.

As I was talking to Jack, the back wheel of John's motorcycle hit a patch of oil and he skidded helplessly along the elevated section of the M4 motorway in west London.

The cartoons on the television had finished and Sunday's religious programmes were failing to hold the children's attention. John should have been home ages ago. Jack's words were beginning to worry me but what could I do? I thought of phoning the police, but I could hardly say: 'Excuse me, my two-and-a-half-year old has told me my husband has gone poly-boys on his motorcycle . . . somewhere between London and Reading.' So I abandoned that idea and reasoned that toddlers were always predicting someone's downfall. This must be Jack's way of projecting his hostile feelings against his father, who had perhaps denied him a second ice cream the day before. Or perhaps he was talking about something he'd seen on television.

By 11 o'clock the baby was howling, the children had eaten the entire week's supply of biscuits and, fearing the worst, I had started planning the tea after the funeral service, when I heard John's bike and rushed out. 'I know what's happened,' I cried, 'Jack told me.' I looked at the battered bike and rider with a mixture of fury, relief and amazement.

John had not been killed, although he could easily have been. At that time on a Sunday morning the usually chaotic M4, the main motorway westward out of London, was not teeming with traffic. Only his pride and his beloved Honda VF750 had been hurt.

Later we discussed the incident and tried to find a rational explanation. Was Jack a seer? He had never shown any trace of other-worldliness, neither then nor now. He was a perfectly ordinary, scruffy, noisy little boy whose only accurate prophecy in the past had been: 'Daddy be cross about the sand.' This was after he had just shovelled the entire contents of his sand pit through the dining room window while pretending to be an excavator on a building site!

Had it all happened as I remembered it? Memory, even for recent events, can be very unreliable and we are remarkably prone to recall as a fact what was merely suggested. Quite unconsciously, in retelling a story even a few minutes later, we add details, exclude some which we might think irrelevant and tidy up the incident, not intending fraud but simply to try to make sense of what happened in our own terms. This has been proved in psychological experiments when subjects have watched a film of say a car accident. Less than half an hour later, it has been remarkably easy to convince the viewers that the car passed a non-existent barn or stopped at a Give Way rather than a Stop sign. This process is intensified under real conditions of stress.

Did Jack really say that daddy had had an accident or did he merely imply it? Had John not had an accident, would I have recalled merely an unfulfilled hint or nothing at all? After all how many times a day does a child predict something that does not come true? Any harassed mother will confirm that the figure could run into hundreds. So the occasional hit is inevitable and at the age of two-and-a-half, mummy and daddy are likely to feature a great deal in a child's fantasies.

Had it just been a coincidence? I was always worried about John driving home when he was very tired and perhaps Jack had voiced my fear then tried to reassure me by saying his daddy would be all right. He might have made similar remarks before that I had not consciously registered and it was only when John was late and I was searching for an explanation that I recalled this one.

But the question remains: did John at the moment of his accident send out some signal that Jack, who was especially close to him, picked up? Was it some form of telepathy? The accident happened on 4 January 1987. At the time of writing, November 1989, we are still not sure what happened.

Some people we told about the incident immediately seized the rational options. Others said that it was a well-known fact that children were psychic but offered little evidence for this statement. More interesting were those who, sometimes hesitantly, told us of strange occurrences involving their childhood or their children.

One such story came from a colleague of my husband, John Keeble. He was aviation correspondent with the *Evening News* in London in 1975 and his job often took him away from home. He was covering a story in Hong Kong when, at about two in the morning, he woke with a strong sensation that something was dreadfully wrong and he had to phone home. He eventually gave in to the impulse and phoned home to find that his son, Simon, then aged three, had caught his arm on a piece of wood while playing and trapped a splinter in the muscle. The boy was taken to hospital where he was operated on and had to stay overnight.

At that stage in his career, John Keeble was used to being away from home and was not given to ringing up whenever he felt uneasy. But on this occasion the feeling was so strong, he could not resist it. Nothing like it has happened before or since, he says. Until then he had been highly sceptical of the occult and allied subjects, having had to deal with numerous reports of flying saucers and the like. He still feels sceptical about many aspects but this was an incident for which he could not easily find an explanation.

But these stories alone are not convincing proof of telepathy for most of the serious scientists who bother to deal with the subject. They demand proof from experiments which can be reproduced in a laboratory, ideally over and over again, in the same way that the laws of physics can be proved. The most popular experiments – with the scientists if not the participants – involve telepathic 'receivers' trying to guess what cards are being turned over by telepathic 'senders'. To be of any statistical use, the cards must be turned over hundreds and hundreds of times. We hardly bothered to weigh up the possibility of testing Jack's telepathic powers in this way. The likelihood of engaging Jack's attention in a card turning experiment for even a few minutes was slim.

Even if we could have got him interested, past experiments have proved that card prediction is pretty boring and that bored children can come up with some ingenious forms of cheating. The other problem is that in a laboratory there can be little of the emotional links, hopes and fears that seem to drive the force known as telepathy.

Anyway, we had no laboratory for setting up elaborate experiments. But we did have something better when John replaced the battered Honda with a BMW 650. 'German engineering is so much more solid,' he told me in an attempt to calm my fears. 'I'll be much safer.' I was still worried about accidents, but I suppose from a purely scientific viewpoint I should have been glad and seen that John's love of two-wheeled transport and the number of lunatics on the road might provide the possibility of history repeating itself and Jack getting another crack at receiving a message from a 'daddy going poly-boys'. But this time, having had a go at telepathy, Jack tried something new.

One evening in November 1988, when Miranda was almost three, but our fifth child Bill who was eight months old had filled the nightly teething spot, Jack began talking about a daddy being involved in a motorcycle accident. This time he did not speak as if he was picking up some strong emotion from an actual incident. It was more of a fairground prediction. It was about 7 o'clock in the evening, and he was not watching television where he might have picked up the idea, but demolishing his younger sister's Lego model. His words were vague and I was not even sure he was talking about our daddy, though he said the daddy had a beard, which ours did.

John was now working on the *Guardian* newspaper in London and we were still living near Reading, so I rang his office to check that he had arrived safely. He had so I asked if in his office there were any daddies, or adults that Jack might class as daddies, who had arrived in a battered state after their bike was hit by a van or lorry on a 'stiff road' near an office where there was a tower 'where people went up and down'. John knew of no such accidents, then, worried about his deadlines, rang off after assuring me that he would be extra careful on his way home. But he did find time to complain that Jack's warning had been a bit light on detail. I then tried to question Jack about the crash, but he was remarkably uncooperative in supplying more information, obviously feeling that he had done his bit already. 'You know,' he said impatiently, 'you know!' Apparently, the 'daddy' had been hit by a lorry but had not fallen off, but was it our 'daddy' or another 'daddy' and where had this happened? 'On the stiff road,' Jack replied impatiently. He knew perfectly well what a 'stiff' road was and saw no reason to explain it to thick adults. It was 'near daddy's work' and 'the tower where people go up and down,' of course. The ancient oracles that spoke in riddles would have been proud of Jack.

That night John arrived home later than usual, not because the prophecy had come true but because he had driven more carefully than usual. Though a bit of a sceptic, he admitted to taking extra care when passing several towers on his way back: the Post Office Tower, the neogothic architecture of St Pancras railway station and hotel blocks near Heathrow airport just off the M4. Furthermore, although he knew there was nothing in it, he had kept a sharp lookout for lorries.

Nothing happened for the next few days so we began to wonder if by 'daddy' Jack had meant somebody else's daddy or just any grown-up, or perhaps no one at all. After all, we knew that the picture of a motorcycle accident was already in Jack's mind. A few weeks before, we had seen one involving a motorcyclist with a beard, just like his father. This made quite an impression on Jack and he talked a lot about ambulances and blood and squashed people – he was not particularly upset but quite interested by the idea.

Then, some three weeks later, on Wednesday 30 November 1988, John was driving back from London along the M4 at about 70mph when he saw a bunch of slower cars ahead. He decelerated to match their speed but the butcher's van racing up behind him didn't. There was a sickening jolt as the van smacked into the back of the bike and John shot forward like a bullet from a gun. If he had come off at that speed on the motorway in traffic, he might have been killed. But John hung on and managed to brake just before hitting the cars ahead.

You could say that Jack had done it again, only this time he'd seen into the future. There had been a van or lorry in the accident and daddy had stayed on and was not hurt. Again we tried to find the rational explanation. Given the high number of road accidents involving motorcyclists and the number of accidents on the M4 – one of the most dangerous motorways in Britain – which John travelled along twice a day, four or five times a week usually when tired, the chances of a mishap were very high. So perhaps Jack's 'gypsy's warning' had a fairly high chance of coming true.

And what about the tower that Jack mentioned? At the scene of the accident, near the M25 interchange, the nearest towers are at Heathrow and are well out of sight. The stiff road might mean the motorway but it could mean anything – roadworks, an elevated section – you pays your money and you takes your choice. Jack at different times would imply that the road was where broken cars were, or it was the dual carriageway, but if he bothered to actually answer questions about it at all he just said: 'You know, the stiff road.'

But although there are some unexplained points in his prediction a lot of it was accurate. Jack, if he could, might argue: 'I said daddy would be hit by a van and not come off the bike. He was hit and he didn't come off. Tell any motorcyclist about this accident and watch them turn white. Ask them what the odds are of staying on in a crash like that. If the van hadn't hit daddy in exactly the right place at the right speed he would have spun off to the side and gone straight under the wheels of the traffic behind.'

Later, while researching this book, I discussed both the cases involving Jack with Janet Boucher, a child psychiatrist, who wondered whether they were Jack's way of trying to tell his father he was worried about him riding the motorbike. She said that often children fear for their parents' safety, but do not know how to express it. As a child, she remembered always being terrified that her father would be involved in a train crash on the way to work but was never able to confide these fears to her mother. However, Jack loves motorcycles – 'When I'm a daddy, I'll have a motorbike for work' is a constant refrain. It might be a form of whistling in the dark to deny his hidden fears but this seems very unlikely.

Laboratory experiments may have failed to come up with convincing proof of children's psychic abilities, but children have traditionally been regarded as having second sight. Until the mid-nineteenth century, young boys would travel round Europe interpreting the crystal ball for their frequently fraudulent masters. In ancient Greece, young boys were used for 'scrying' – divining the future by gazing into bowls of pure water lit by burning torches. They studied the changes in the water in the flickering light and invoked the gods or demons to provide a meaning. Cagliostro, the eighteenth-century magician and adventurer, is reported to have often used young children to help him predict the future or perform acts of clairvoyance. In one famous incident, the five-year-old son of Marshal von Medem, under Cagliostro's guidance, saw the unexpected arrival home of his elder brother and was able to describe what was going on in other rooms of the house.

In modern western society, it is no longer normal to invoke the 'sight' professionally from children (however, a psychic counsellor called Lilian has told me how she had her own clientele for tea leaf readings when she was small but her story will be told in another chapter). But it seems children's predictions are nonetheless quite common and sometimes accurate. Are they less aware of the limitations of time and space, more instinctive or simply less hesitant than adults about speaking out and perhaps getting it wrong?

Jack's apparent telepathic link with his father during a time of stress is mirrored by a story told about the late Sir Peter Scott, the naturalist, painter and sailor. When he was a young child, about the time his father, Captain Scott, died in the Antarctic in his bid to reach the South Pole, he is said to have told his mother: 'Daddy's stopped working.'

I asked him about the story shortly before his death in 1989 and Sir Peter wrote back: 'The story you describe was related to me in later years by my mother who was very loath to believe that it had any significance, as she was always very sceptical of psychic phenomena. But the fact that she told me the story indicates, I think, that she was unwilling to dismiss the incident. I'm afraid I do not

recall the actual happening at all. Nor do I remember any
other such phenomena in my childhood. But, as in so
many other fields, I like to think I keep an open mind.'

Did the boy in fact share his father's last moments or
did he often talk about his father and sometimes, as many
children do, play at being his father, so that perhaps he
was acting out some of the anxieties that had been expressed about the dangerous nature of his father's mis-
sion?

Sir Peter's mother, Kathleen Bruce, the sculptress who
was to create the famous Peter Pan statue that stands in
Kensington Gardens (J. M. Barrie, author of *Peter Pan* was
Sir Peter Scott's godfather) had no inkling of her husband's death and it was six months before the frozen
bodies of Scott and his companions were discovered. But
there is evidence that as death approached Captain Scott
was thinking of his family. Among the letters he wrote
during the time he was awaiting death in the snowbound
tent, was one to J.M. Barrie saying: 'I want you to help my
widow and my son, your godson . . . Give the boy a chance
in life if the state won't do it – he ought to have good stuff
in him.'

Sir Peter was certainly an exceptional person, but
whenever I relate the story of Jack I am surprised at the
number of mothers of perfectly ordinary children who
come out with extraordinary tales of their offspring's
psychic experiences ranging from minor cases of telepathy to poltergeists. Usually these stories are kept
under cover for fear of ridicule or worse. In nearly all the
stories that follow, the names have been changed and
details disguised at the request of the tellers, some of
whom, even years later feel insecure about discussing

their experiences.

Many children have been through experiences that their parents just dismissed as fantasy. Christine, now an adult, told me that she always knew when things were going to happen but her mother would not believe that this came from any paranormal ability and accused her of listening at doors. One child psychiatrist told me that he had never heard a child tell him about ghosts. It could be because such incidents were rare, but as he pointed out: 'The child may well not tell you things like that. The child may well be frightened that he is going mad or may be seen that way. Also it can worry the mother who may encourage the child to keep quiet about that aspect of family life.' As one mother said: 'I just knew the psychologist would label us straight away so I told my child not to mention it.'

Michael Jackson, a psychologist working at the Alister Hardy Research Centre for Religious and Spiritual Experiences in Oxford, considers that badly-handled childhood psychic experiences can make the child withdraw from reality and perhaps lead to later mental problems. He considers that sensitive people are most likely to have such experiences and so will be even more hurt if these experiences are rejected. Certainly adults can react very negatively towards children who do not conform.

One of the saddest cases I have heard of was that of Carol who, when little, used to talk to animals and people whom even her twin sister could not see. Eventually she mentioned a Red Indian chief she used to see and her parents got so worried that they had her taken to a mental hospital when she was a teenager. There she realised that if she was going to get out she had to play by the rules.

She no longer mentioned the things although she kept seeing them. When she was 25 she went to a medium who told her that she was psychic and had a Red Indian guide. Carol has never forgiven her parents for what they did. Even now, although she holds a responsible job, her parents refuse to discuss either what happened or anything to do with her psychic experiences.

Children are much more vulnerable than adults who have learned, in Carol's phrase, 'to play by the rules'. If an adult sees what might be a ghost or experiences what might be telepathy, he or she will usually either rationalise it or keep quiet. But children open their mouths hoping to be believed or reassured and all too often are ignored or frightened. The adult code of silence extends even to people connected with organisations which investigate the paranormal. They have told me stories about psychic experiences of their childhood or that of their relatives then quickly said: 'But if you use it, don't mention my name as it's not fair to my family.' Telepathy, ghosts and things that go bump in the night are fine in stories or fables. In everyday life, they can start off all sorts of ripples, which can be a real threat to the picture of the safe old world, sanitised and technologically in order.

Children already cause enough disorder in everyday life, as any parent or aunt or uncle knows. Mix them with the paranormal and the results can be shattering. When I started off to write a nice neat book about the psychic power of children, I found that the stories I gathered would not fit into nice neat packages any more than children will fit into their nice neat clothes on those important occasions when you want them to look their best.

Children's psychic experiences start where fantasy begins and ends – who knows where? For that reason, I have included some of the borderline stories of children's invisible friends, magic lands and night terrors and readers must make up their own minds which side of the boundaries of imagination they lie. More often than not the children themselves cannot distinguish between the paranormal and fantasy and may accept the verdict of adults that they have been dreaming. Only in later life do they look back and say: 'I didn't realise at the time, but it was not mere fantasy as I was told. It was an actual psychic experience.' For some old people those magic moments of childhood have proved to be more important than the rest of their lives put together. For that reason I have included their reminiscences.

Also included are the stories of adults who have had paranormal experiences involving children. For children do not live alone and often their 'magic' can rub off on mothers, fathers, relatives – and even teachers. From the moment a baby arrives in the world – some would say even before then – the effect on those around can be startling. I got some amazing stories from the National Childbirth Trust and La Leche Breastfeeding League – not at all the sort of people you'd expect to come out with paranormal stories. But they knew exactly what I was talking about. A bond beyond our normal understanding between mother and baby appeared to save a child's life in several cases. This tie might fade as the child grows but sometimes even a six-foot tall seventeen-year-old will send out a mental distress signal that the mother picks up.

Occasionally, I have been told that a child's mother is

also psychic and even that the grandmother and often the great-grandparents were too. This is where things can get really complicated. I have been told of a relatively simple incident then spent another three hours trying to unravel the psychic family tree! But mainly I have written about ordinary people with ordinary children who have had out-of-the-ordinary things happen to them. I have also consulted the archives at the Alister Hardy Research Centre in Oxford and the International Association for Near Death Studies at Northleach to see how widespread psychic phenomena are and to make sure that I didn't just happen to know a lot of funny people.

Before my experience with Jack I would have been tempted to discard many of the stories I came across as an insult to common sense. Now I feel that they need more careful study and have included them. Always names and details have been changed, as requested by the people and institutes I spoke to, to protect the tellers from scorn or ridicule.

I talked to psychiatrists, psychotherapists and family therapists to see how they would interpret children's paranormal experiences. Stress in a family, especially at a time of separation or bereavement, and the psychological make-up of a child are bound to influence the way he or she makes sense of a situation. The psychological workers came up with some fascinating alternative explanations that are well worth consideration, but although psychology might explain away some things, often there are still gaps in our knowledge.

Whether the incidents are psychological or psychic, in my view the most important factor is how an incident involving children has made people look at the world in a different light. The purpose of the psychic power of children could be to add a new dimension to everyday half-forgotten experiences and to make us question, with the open mind of a child, our reason for being here.

2

Telepathic Links

Jack's little bit of telepathy with his motorcycling father (we have not yet been able to come up with a better explanation for this incident) occurred at a moment of stress for the family and for John. Telepathy under stress is a difficult subject to study systematically because crises cannot happen to order and certainly not just to oblige the ever-eager psychologist or scientist. But it is possible to look at telepathic experiences, talk to those involved, find out something of the context in which the events occurred and to look at underlying feelings. These experiences usually seem to involve close relatives. Do their minds become attuned so that a physical presence is not necessary to communicate in times of strong emotions and a kind of psychic SOS is sent out?

During the retreat to Dunkirk in the last world war, Michael, a young army officer, was killed. Back home, in the countryside near Ipswich, his daughter Fiona was living with her grandmother, aunts and mother. She told them: 'Daddy came to me last night and told me to take care of mummy.' Next day, a telegram brought the news that her father had been killed.

Stories of premonitions and visitations abound in time of war when there is also the increased probability of a child's fears of a parent's death, voiced at random, becoming reality. When father is away, the prospect of the telegram is not a vague fantasy. Children pick up chance remarks, unspoken glances and unfinished sentences. They may project fears about who will take care of mummy into dreams – perhaps not remembered, perhaps not reported, perhaps not always heard by adults. We do not often attend to what children say. When we do, it can be a shock.

Was Fiona trying to make sense of a world where daddy had gone away and might not come back? Perhaps she dreamed of the father she was missing and that he was telling her to be a good girl. Many fathers, even if they are only going on the 8.15 to Waterloo, say to a child, 'Take care of mummy while I'm away.' The child who is still linked closely to the mother feels responsible. The father's absence may also strengthen the existing fear in all young children that mummy too may go – an anxiety that most psychologists recognise in one way or another.

Freud said that young children often believe they have the power to destroy a parent by bad thoughts and so repress these thoughts, only to have them surface in sleep or fantasy play. He himself felt very guilty over the death of his fifteen-month-old brother Julius because he was jealous of him. He felt his thoughts were almost magical in their power and the totally unconnected death of Julius seemed to confirm this. So a child may rehearse his or her worst fears in sleep or play to lessen their impact. But in Fiona's case it may be that the adults imbued her words with unearned significance. Or perhaps she really did sense something had happened.

Were Michael's last thoughts for the wife and child he would never see again and did these emotions reach his child as she slept, when her conscious barriers were down and she would have been at her most receptive? But what matters more than whether the experience was paranormal, is the function it served. It was in a way a preparation for the bad news and above all a positive statement, whether or not borne out in what scientists call hard facts, that Michael loved his family to the end.

Conversely can a child project his dying thoughts to his parents? Sandra woke in the middle of the night with the most terrible pain in her stomach. She staggered to the bathroom, but by the time she got there the pain had vanished. A few hours later she heard that her teenage son Gifford had been involved in an accident on his motorbike. He had come off and been hit in the stomach by a road sign. He was dead on arrival in hospital.

Did Sandra share her son's pain? She had no premonition of disaster and no inkling of why she suffered a sudden and passing agony. She was devastated, but she was able to take some comfort from the belief that if the terrible pain she had experienced a few hours earlier had only lasted a few seconds, her son had only suffered for a very short time. Gifford's elder sister, who told me the story, said that often there is the very real worry that though doctors may say a person only suffered for a very short time, they may just be saying that for the benefit of the relatives.

An American, Lucille Hurd, provides another example of a mother feeling her child's distress, even 3,000 miles away on the other side of the United States. When she was a child, her father used to drive passengers across America. Sometimes he invited Lucille and her mother to come with him but it involved travelling 600 miles a day for 30 days and her mother, who had made the crossing several times, hated it. On one particular occasion she decided to stay behind but let Lucille go along with her father and grandfather. This was Lucille's third trip and she and her grandfather and father were sitting in the front with three passengers in the back. 'On the journey to California, the car went off the road and turned over – I thought at that terrifying moment of my mother 3,000 miles away in Baltimore. Next morning we phoned her from Yakima and the instant she heard my voice, she cried, "How are you? – My God, I saw you turned over in a ditch in my dream. Are they treating you well in the clinic?"'

The passengers in the back seat were hurt and had to stay in hospital. But Lucille, her father and grandfather were only shaken and were discharged from hospital almost straight away.

As the young Lucille was travelling thousands of miles by car, it is not unexpected that her mother would be anxious and could dream of a car crash. She had made the trip and so she could clearly picture the hazards on the road. She might also have been worried that her daughter was homesick. Perhaps she was feeling guilty and felt she should have gone along, thinking 'Supposing she was badly hurt and I was not there.' On the other hand she was right about the car turning over and going into a ditch.

Janette recalls how when her second son Damien was about four, her husband took him and his six-year-old brother Daniel to the swimming pool. 'After about 30 minutes, I looked at the clock. It was 2.48 pm and I had a feeling something had happened to Damien. I remember I kept thinking of him with a bandage round his forehead. As time wore on, I was quite convinced he'd bumped his forehead. When they returned later, Damien got out of the car with a sort of white netting bandage on his head, like a cap but almost falling over his eyes. He had cracked the back of his head open on a metal bar and had had 12 stitches, but being on the back of his head they had to bandage right round to keep the dressing in place. The time the accident happened, my husband said, was nearly ten to three.'

Telepathic messages need not always be about death and disaster but can surface perhaps at times of domestic crises. Ann says: 'I was at a keep fit class with my two younger children when I suddenly felt I had to leave. I gathered the children up and drove home. As I turned the corner into my road, I saw my sixteen-year-old, Pam, and two friends leaving my house loaded with bags and I realised she was leaving home. We had not argued, but she felt that at sixteen she wanted to be independent. I was able to go after her and persuade her not to go at that point. She has since left, but to a far better situation than the one she was going to then. If I had not left the class at that point she would have been gone when I left home and things would have turned out very differently.'

Was this a lucky coincidence or had Ann picked up some unconscious signals from earlier signs Pam had displayed? Or was Pam unconsciously calling for help to stop her from taking a step she was perhaps already regretting but unable to turn back from for fear of losing face. Is telepathy between parent and child an extension of the ability of a ewe to pick out its lambs bleat in a whole field or a mother to identify her newborn's cry from all others?

Sisters may have a special bond. Doris was fourteen and taking care of her younger sisters who were eleven and seven, while their mother had gone shopping. The house was one of the old back-to-back type in Salford with a black kitchen range and an open fire in the living room. 'My mother would often leave a pan to cook on the fire. I went upstairs, leaving my sisters together. I heard my middle sister call my name with great urgency. As my name was called I saw what was taking place downstairs – the pan of soup on the fire had been knocked by my youngest sister and the contents were pouring over her legs. I came down the stairs finding what I had expected, pulled my sister away from the fire as she still sat there shocked and in pain. Afterwards my middle sister remarked that I had not asked her what had happened, but simply came down and did what was necessary. She asked me how I had known.'

Had Doris not acted so promptly, the situation could have been far worse. The argument for some kind of telepathy has to be balanced by the argument that often certain dangers are in the back of one's mind at all times and that a call for help can invoke the reaction 'Oh Lord, I knew that would happen!' Doris must have had at the back of her mind the dangers of the range. What is interesting is the calm way in which she reacted to a crisis and not panicking as many would do if their worst fears were confirmed. 'Seeing' the situation might have helped her stay cool.

But sometimes the person who 'sees' the situation can be ignored, with tragic consequences. Helen, who lives on Merseyside and has four children, was in bed with a migraine one evening. But at about 10 o'clock, she got up and insisted the whole family dressed so that they could go round to one of her sisters because she had a dreadful feeling there was something very wrong with one of the children. When they arrived, Helen found the baby was feverish and asked her sister to call the doctor. Her sister refused, saying: 'I've had four children. I know when one's ill.' The baby was later diagnosed as suffering from meningitis from which he has never fully recovered.

It is the sense of urgency that seems to single out what are apparently telepathic feelings from other less specific anxieties. But there is a second kind of telepathy which can take place in a completely relaxed situation often when parent and child are travelling. However, the child, having seen what is in the parent's mind might well demand urgent action. And that is when the trouble starts.

Carla has four children, so moments without them are very precious. One day she was pushing the baby in the pushchair and Dylan, who was aged about four was trotting along beside her. Suddenly she thought: 'Oh, I'll take the kids home and change into my old red cords and slip round on my bike to see mum. It doesn't matter what I look like.' She was standing at the crossroads at this point and told me that she had a very clear picture in her mind of herself on her bike pedalling round to her mother's. At almost the same moment Dylan looked up and said crossly: 'Mum, why are you going on your bike in your red trousers to see nan and not taking me?'

The limpet has much to learn from the average toddler about togetherness. These days I rarely have a bath without Bill and Miranda joining me, Jack hurling toy ducks and Tom and Jade popping in and out chatting or demanding I referee the latest dispute. Is it any wonder that children can anticipate our every word and potential movement? Yet Dylan not only knew his mother was planning to make a bid for freedom, he pictured the bike and the red cords at almost the same moment Carla did.

Travel featured in several experiences which were related to me, as did a state of relaxed silence between the transmitter and receiver. In 1964, Doris was sitting on a train in Manchester with her four-year-old daughter Susan on their way to see Doris's mother. 'We were waiting for the train to leave the station,' said Doris. 'Susan was looking at a comic and I was daydreaming. We were both silent. My thoughts went back to a journey I had made many years before when I was living in a house at Bosham Bay in Sussex. I had been on a trip to London and my feet were tired. On arriving at Bosham station, I took off my shoes to walk home. Now sitting on the train in Manchester all those years later, I was recalling the exact sensation of walking down the bay road without shoes and the feel of the road under my stockinged feet, when Susan looked up from her comic and said: "Why do you never let me walk down the road without shoes?"'

Doris says she and Susan have retained their telepathic link even though Susan is now grown up. Was Doris unconsciously wriggling her feet or had she, even without realising, half slipped off her shoes and thereby triggered off a thought in her daughter's mind that she also would like not to wear shoes? The incident remains intriguing.

Judith was driving with her two-and-a-half year old son Malcolm to her part-time job. 'It was a very cold winter when there was a lot of hoar frost and the journey along country roads took longer than usual. As we drove along, I was remembering how I used to spend a lot of time when I was little driving with my father, a GP, on his country practice round in New Zealand. I remembered watching his gloved hands on the steering wheel and I was thinking how my experience must have been very similar to Malcolm's now. We were driving in silence when Malcolm suddenly said, "You are daddy in Scotland." By this he meant my father who by this time had retired to the Scottish Highlands, where the children and I often went to stay with him. Malcolm's own father had only once been to Scotland with us and we lived in Royston in Hertfordshire, so I think he was quite clear who he meant. We would often talk of going to Grandpa in Scotland.'

Perhaps Malcolm associated driving for what seemed a long time with mummy not daddy in the car and with going to Scotland. It is hard when children come out with such remarks to trace the actual association. Sometimes, like Chinese whispers, this can be incredibly complex. But again, it occurred in the silent time when conscious thought was not intruding. Perhaps a mother's mind, when the thoughts and images in it are vivid enough, becomes like a screen on which a child can see pictures.

Jeanne has had experience of telepathy on the move and at home. She told me that on the first occasion she had just moved to Guernsey from London and William, their first-born was three years old. 'I had received a letter from my friend and neighbour in London and she had mentioned a woman whom she thought I knew – Simon's mother. I could not think who she meant and kept saying to myself – entirely in my head – "Simon, who is Simon?" I had not actually uttered a word when William, who was in the same room, said to me: "You know Simon, mummy. He was my friend."'

On the second occasion she was in the back of the car with their second son Thomas who was four. Their third child had just been born and she was thinking to herself about the possibility of a fourth child when Thomas piped up: 'Would four be enough mummy?' 'Four what?' she asked, somewhat startled. 'Four children, of course,' he replied.

Jeanne is certain that on neither of these occasions did she voice her thoughts aloud, although she admits she was thinking in word form and the thoughts were very simple. So if the potential for telepathy is there these conditions were probably ideal for it. Also there was nothing else happening at the time. Jeanne also mentioned: 'On other occasions I have suspected that something was going on, but the evidence was not so clear. I have also tried to make it happen but have never succeeded as far as I know.'

Jeanne may have been certain that she did not voice her thoughts aloud but some parents drop into the habit of keeping up a running commentary of their actions (like their children do) and do not realise they are doing it. 'Oh look! A train!' I once loudly informed the startled passengers on a bus. I had forgotten that for once I did not have a child with me to tell about the train. One executive

I know announced at a board meeting when coffee was wheeled in: 'Oh good, bickies!' Many parents unconsciously carry on a kind of burble without realising and thus impart information to a child. Then they are amazed when the child appears to know their 'secret' thoughts.

The other interesting point that Jeanne raises is that when she deliberately tried to use telepathy the children could not or would not cooperate which is bad news for the scientific community.

As mentioned in the first chapter, a lot of experiments have been carried out to test for telepathic ability in children and the results have either been very poor or have simply demonstrated the ingenuity of children in devising amazing codes of sniffs, shuffles, coughs and chair-creaking in the interests of improving their results, if only to get the whole thing over and done with! Dr Ernesto Spinelli, however, did carry out some tests with children as young as three that seemed to show that small children had considerable telepathic powers. He found that three-year-olds did best of all, but the apparent ability declined from then on until at the age of eight when the results, like those of adults, were the same as chance guessing.

Dr Spinelli found that results were best when the children tested together were the same age and even better, when their IQs were the same. His interpretation of his experiments would seem to indicate that telepathic powers come from the same source as ordinary thought, but that in a young child this ability has not yet been suppressed by learning. Telepathic powers, he believes, are a sort of externalised thinking that disappears once a child learns to keep his thinking inside his head.

Commenting on the relaxation factor involved in real

life telepathy he told me: 'My own feelings are that this is linked with the limitations of self-consciousness that are typically imposed, but which become more blurred when one is in a relaxed, meditative or altered state. Since young children are only just beginning to have a clearly defined sense of self, it is possible that their superior ability at telepathic tasks is a reflection of their comparative open self-consciousness. Telepathy only strikes adults as odd or unusual because they have a strong sense of self-consciousness – a notion that our thoughts are ours and ours alone.'

Dr Spinelli's experiments were carried out some 10 years ago and so far no one has managed to get the same results. Instead people have been more interested in finding fault with his work, rather than building on it and investigating a potentially very rich field.

I am not sure where Sarah, now a clairvoyant and medium, fits into Dr Spinelli's theory, but she says her brother, who was four years younger than her, did not learn to speak till he was three and a half, because she knew exactly what he wanted and would interpret for him. This is not uncommon. My own older children have interpreted their younger siblings' seemingly meaningless babble for me with great success. But Sarah says she could also tell as a child what people were saying when they were having a conversation some distance away. At first she thought she just had good hearing, but then realised that such ability would have been impossible unless she was a bat.

Telepathy between parent and child is not restricted to mothers. On several occasions Tasha has felt she and her father can read each other's minds. Once they were in the car together and, as Tasha told me: 'I was wondering if friends of mine, Malcolm and Maxie, were coming to our barbecue. I didn't say anything. I was just thinking, when out of the blue dad said, "No, I don't think so. Mum forgot to invite them."'

In some children, telepathic ability is not restricted to family but can extend at random to complete strangers. Adam who is twelve told me: 'When I was ten, I was on the tube in London with my mum. There was a big man standing next to me. I asked him where he came from and he said America. Then I asked him if he played a flute and he was amazed. "Yes," he said, "How did you know?" I said I just did.' Adam says there were no apparent signs that the man was a musician. It is hard to imagine a non-verbal cue that would have narrowed down the instrument that the man played, even had he been humming or tapping out a rhythm with his feet.

Another time Adam was at the Chalk Pits in Hampshire where he had gone to see the Bhundu Boys. A man next to him boasted he was psychic and could tell fortunes. Adam had heard the man say to his friend that he had a boat and decided to have a bit of fun. 'You've got a boat,' he said. 'Yes,' replied the man, 'but what colour is it?' 'Blue and white,' said Adam, without knowing how he had come to the correct answer. This might have been just a lucky guess – blue and white is a fairly common colour combination for boats but he went on to tell the man he had a former girlfriend called Emma who was interested in politics. The so-called psychic was amazed and told Adam to go on, but he couldn't.

Adam recalls another occasion on the beach at Paignton when he told his mum: 'That girl's called Jan, I think.'

The next minute the girl's friend came up and said: 'Hello Jan.' Adam says it just sometimes happens that he knows something, but he can't make it happen. This would fit in with the theory that telepathic ability, if it exists, only occurs spontaneously and is therefore not potentially testable without altering the nature of the phenomena being measured.

It is often very easy to believe that a telepathic experience has taken place. When my husband is at home in the evenings (not very often with his job) I push our insomniac youngest son Bill round the local roads at about 10 o'clock at night. One evening, we passed a garden with a cat sitting on the lawn in the gloom. Bill spotted it and said, 'Hello'. The next evening as we were passing the same house, I was idly wondering if the cat would be there again. At this point Bill pointed at the lawn and said, 'Hello', but the cat was not there. All the houses in the road (and indeed within about five square miles) look the same, so Bill either has a remarkable sense of geography for a 20-month-old or he picked up my thoughts at a time when we were both relaxed and quiet. But am I sure it was the same house or did a random 'hello' from Bill trigger off the association in my mind which later reversed the events and made me think that I had thought about the cat first? Or did I pause at the house and look expectantly, so that Bill felt there must be something around worth saying hello to?

Telepathy can have its uses for parents. Some believe they are able to will their children to sleep. Wendy writes of the sleepless nights she had in 1980 with her son William. 'One night as the familiar crying noises began, my husband and I both stirred into semi-consciousness at the same time. Once he began to wake up, William rarely subsided until he had been fed and we both groaned as we were pretty exhausted. Still only half awake, I said, "Quick, let's think him back to sleep." This we both did and within a short time William was soundly sleeping.' Wendy is convinced, however, that she can only do this in a half-conscious state because if she was awake enough to do it deliberately then she would realise it was not possible.

Tim also tells me that he used to tune into his elder daughter Hannah when she was a restless baby and will her to stop crying and go back to sleep. Tim thinks he and Hannah are very alike in temperament. He says: 'If Doro, my wife, went to Hannah, she would insist on a feed, so I used to get up instead. I would visualise Hannah in bed and picture her head, beaming in on her from our bedroom. This beaming went on until Hannah was almost two, sometimes as many as five times a night. Tim says it didn't work every time, but it often did because he believed it would. He feels this homing in on Hannah forged telepathic bonds that still exist between them.

Colin Wilson, the author and expert on the paranormal, mentions similar telepathic links with his children in his book *The Occult* and describes elaborate precautions he had to take so that they would not wake up. This included not thinking about his daughter before he went to sleep in case she picked up his thoughts. Hypnosis is, in fact, based on not dissimilar principles and as one psychic counsellor pointed out to me, people were once burned at the stake for practising hypnotherapy. Witchcraft still does not have a very good reputation but I, and thousands of other parents of tiny insomniacs, would be

grateful for a foolproof spell or two for getting our little
. . . dears . . . to sleep.

3

Mother and Child Bonding

A special form of telepathic link appears to exist between mothers and their newly-born (and sometimes unborn) infants. Many woman say they wake the second before their baby cries and 'sit bolt upright in bed', though they may sleep through an older child's yells. Or they will somehow sense their baby is in distress. Yet these women were not telepathic or psychic before. The difference appears to be that they are linked to the child and because that child is not yet fully emotionally or psychologically separate, it can transmit his or her psychic energy to and through the mother so that she can for a brief time share the child's needs and emotions. What is commonly disregarded as just a mother/baby thing may be one of the most exciting psychic stages.

The mother's 'ability' seems to relate only to her and the baby, though in some cases the bond appears to remain with one particular child even into adulthood. The baby can and regularly does communicate his needs to his mother through channels that are beyond normal communication. How this works is not fully understood but it does seem to work.

According to Sandra it averted what would otherwise have been a cot death. When Katie was six and a half weeks old, she was quite dozy one day where normally she was demanding. The health visitor had been in for a minor problem and declared everything was fine. 'But all day I felt something was going to happen and I had the irrational thought that if something was going to happen with the baby, I'd rather it happened there and then than later. Geoff, my husband, put her to bed and she settled straight down. But I still felt uneasy. I went into her room, switched on the light and she blinked. I nearly went out but 30 seconds later she had stopped breathing. The doctor said she had been a near-cot death and we were in hospital for eight days while she was checked over. I have never felt like that before or since. The hospital could find no reason why it had happened. I am very close to Katie, maybe because I breastfed her.'

When Daniel was seven and a half months old, Janette remembers: 'My husband had closed Daniel's bedroom door because he was running a bath and the noise of the water would have woken Daniel. He had his bath and I went to run mine and as I passed the bedroom door I had the overwhelming feeling I had to go to Daniel, so even though the taps were full on and the tank was filling noisily I went straight in to find him choking. He couldn't even cry because he couldn't get enough breath in. We managed to get him to the casualty department of the local hospital. They were able to ventilate him and gave him intravenous antibiotics which fortunately worked quite quickly because his throat was closing due to a serious acute respiratory tract infection. We stayed in hospital five days and came out on Christmas Eve, the best Christmas present we ever had.'

Joanne also believes her nine-week-old son James was saved by the psychic link between them. 'I took him to a friend's house. She had two toddlers so we put James upstairs for his sleep. My friend checked him and came down, but I felt I had to check him again almost straight away. When I went in, he was turning navy blue. I only just saved him. He has now been given an experimental alarm that detects the blood oxygen level, an earlier stage of detection than breathing which is the last thing to go.' On several occasions, Joanne says she has been impelled to check him and has gone in his room just before the alarm went off.

Jane, a health professional who works extensively with mothers and babies, says that because these experiences are not well-documented or researched and worse still not acknowledged, a valuable warning system for babies' health could be lost. Mothers may suddenly feel that they must go to their baby, even though they may have left the child with their partner or a perfectly reliable babysitter and gone off for just a short time, glad of the break.

Helena, a breastfeeding counsellor with the La Leche League, told me how, when her second child Amy was a few months old, her husband Chris had persuaded her to go out for a couple of hours to see some friends for dinner. The babysitter was left with the number to call in case of any emergency and the couple could be back home within a few minutes. 'When it got to about 10 o'clock,' Helena recalls, 'we were sitting around talking and my attention started to wander. I started to get agitated. "I really think we ought to be going," I insisted. But Chris just said, "Well the babysitter's got our number here if there's any problem."' But Helena had to get back as quickly as possible. She cannot remember how they got out. She felt cut off from the outside world thinking only: 'I want to get back to my baby.' They reached home to find the baby crying and the babysitter trying frantically to phone them – Chris had accidentally put two of the numbers in the wrong order.

Stephanie was three months old and still breastfeeding when Isabel left her with a babysitter to go to the cinema with her husband. The baby had been fed at 7.30pm and normally would not wake up again for some hours. When Isabel left the cinema at 10pm, she was not worried. But walking to the car, she experienced the most incredible surge of milk. 'Hurry up,' she said to her husband, 'Stephanie's awake and screaming her head off.' They reached home twenty minutes later, to find Stephanie screaming blue murder having woken twenty minutes before. Had Isabel unconsciously begun thinking about the baby as she came back to the real world after watching the film. Or was there some telepathic call from child to mother?

It is well-known that mothers seem to wake seconds before their baby does, though they will cheerfully sleep through a yelling toddler provided they know the father is on duty. Carla told me that her husband can remember her suddenly sitting bolt upright in bed, eyes wide open and a second later, the baby would wake up. But it would be wrong to assume that these telepathic links automatically exist, even between the most loving parents and their children, and when they do they seem to appear at random and without any control.

When Bill, my fifth child, was just over a year old, he came down with a virus and was put in a room of his own in the baby isolation ward at the local hospital. I stayed with him but at around midnight, the staff nurse persuaded me to go to bed in a parent's room, as Bill was asleep. She promised to wake me the moment he cried. I went to sleep listening to the cries of the small children in the children's ward nearby. By my fifth child, I had learned to sleep through the sound of other children. But some 45 minutes later I woke suddenly. It was Bill, making the noisy snuffling sobs of a sick baby. At first I thought he was in bed with me then I remembered and ran to the isolation unit.

'What's wrong?' asked the nurse. 'It's Bill, he's crying,' I answered. 'No, he's not,' she said, 'I've been next door.'

But in his room, there was Bill crying, not loudly but making the unmistakeable distressed sound of a very hot, sick child. I comforted and fed him and it was only later that I reflected how strange it was I had picked up Bill's cry from so far away. It is a good example of that uncanny link between mothers and children.

Yet on another and perhaps potentially more dangerous occasion, this link failed me completely. That was the day Bill, not eighteen months old but big for his age, was brought to my front door by a neighbour who had found him sitting happily on the top of a pile of sand left by the builders in her front garden. Somehow he had slipped out – perhaps one of my other young children had left the front door open – and decided to go visiting. It was a heart-stopping moment. He had gone without my

knowing it and might have been anywhere. I had been
lucky that he had been very quickly spotted and brought
back. My instinct and telepathy had failed me completely
on this occasion. Sceptics could argue that it failed
because such a power does not exist. But this is pushing
against the weight of the evidence that my research so far
has uncovered.

It could even be argued that it was in Bill's interests not
to transmit any signal to alert me as I might have stopped
what he was doing when he was enjoying himself, obli-
vious of any personal peril. This leads me to the theory
that if telepathic power does exist in children it may be
that as they grow older they start putting some effort into
deliberately cutting it off and shielding their thoughts
from their parents who might curtail their activities for
the totally irrelevant reason – as the children see it – that
they are likely to break their necks!

Carolyn's son Ben is now eleven months old and she returned to work when he was five months old. 'I work full-
time on rotating shifts, morning, evening and nights.
During the day, Ben is perfectly content to be with other
people while I am at work. He is used to being woken up
in the morning and put to bed at night by people other
than me. However when I work nights, despite my putting him to bed for a perfectly normal evening, he seems
to sense when I leave the house and wakes up the moment
I leave for work. My husband usually has a busy night.
This has happened since I first returned to work when
Ben was five months old.'

Jilly told me that most days, she knows when her baby
will wake. 'We have a large garden and a field beyond
with donkeys and a large area for vegetables and soft

fruit. I spend a great deal of time out here and when Adrian is sleeping I use a mobile alarm to save trekking back to the house to see if he's woken up. Many, many times, I feel very strongly that it is time to come in, though he is quiet on the alarm and by the time I've reached the house, he's waking. Sometimes I can hear him waking as I'm walking back to the house.'

With mother/baby telepathy it is impossible to say which of the two is really the psychic one as they interact so closely. The fact that a mother has carried her baby inside her for nine months, makes her very receptive to the child and strong evidence is emerging that human babies are equally attached to their mothers (unlike other creatures such as ducklings which will attach themselves to the first things they see). Even at birth, a human infant is not just an empty, passive creature but a thinking, feeling being who can recognise mother's voice, her face and even her special smell. These abilities are central to early interaction with the mother and seem to develop far earlier than was previously thought. Though the brain has not matured at birth, a baby's ability to form associations seems to begin as early as the first week of life – assuming he or she can be persuaded to stay awake long enough to perform.

Sandra believes that her eldest child Christina shared her last stages of labour when her second child Janette was born. She and Christina, who was nearly two at the time, were very closely bonded, so much so that Sandra had opted for a home birth in order not to have to be separated from her daughter. 'I had a friend who came to sit up with Christina while I was in labour,' she wrote. 'Christina fell asleep early on in the labour leaning against my friend. Later she described to me how half an hour before the birth, Christina, who had been solidly asleep and not moving until this point, began thrashing around as if she was unable to get comfortable.'

Birth does seem to trigger off many strange experiences. It is almost as if some special kind of energy is released or one's sense of reality is suspended. Most women I spoke to had never had feelings like this prior to giving birth and told me that the only psychic experiences they had known were confined to the birth period or just after. Is this a hormonal reaction, 'one of the peculiarities of birth' as one eminent obstetrician put it (not known for his interest in anything other than the physiological aspects of motherhood) or is the child allowing the mother a glimpse into another world?

Clarrie gave birth during the last war when she had been evacuated from London. 'I woke up in the night. There was a moon and it was not dark and facing the window was the figure of a man wearing white – his head was slightly bent back as if in prayer or on sentinel duty. As I looked in astonishment the figure dissolved before my eyes, leaving a wisp of white that looked like a cloud. It was about 12.30 in the morning.' Again birth seems to have triggered off a strange experience. Did she see a doctor and, in the drowsy state that can follow the stress of childbirth, hallucinate that he had faded away? Or was the uncertainty she felt at giving birth in a strange place without support of family such that her mind projected a benign presence to make her feel less alone? Or is it, as seems likely, that in spite of all modern technological wizardry we understand as little about the mysteries of birth as we do about the mysteries of death and that through the child, the mother is able to reach another level of reality?

Gail writes: 'Before my son was born, I never had a psychic experience. But in the first few months after his birth, I kept running into breezes that literally came from nowhere. They were noticeable enough to make me come to a halt. The most surprising was when I was on a staircase with a brick wall running down one side of it. The breeze seemed to come from the wall!'

Sometimes mothers of new babies seem to be linked with other mothers of new babies in a way that breaks through the language barrier. We took our children to Brittany when Jack was six weeks old. Though my French is not very good, my husband found me chatting away to another woman with small children, who was operating the merry-go-round (a common feature of many French towns in summer) in the town square. 'Well,' I said, 'we both had children so it was no problem.' I have heard similar reports from other mothers. A Breton friend who had to take her daughter to Paris for medical treatment found herself in the same ward as an Italian mother. The Italian spoke no French and our friend spoke no Italian but she found herself being used by the doctors to convey details about the Italian child's treatment. 'We were mothers with sick children,' she said, 'so we could communicate.'

It may be fanciful to think that this mother-to-mother bond could also burst through the time barrier and another incident on that same holiday may have been due to nothing more than imagination. At the lovely thirteenth-century chateau of Suscinio in the Rhuys Peninsula, my husband took our two older children off exploring and I was left sitting in one of the rooms of the chateau feeding Jack. It was the end of July and very hot. I looked across the empty room and sitting in a large wooden chair by a fire was a woman in a long dress nursing her baby. I felt she could see me and I could see her. It was as if we were on different sides of a thick sheet of glass. I did not feel scared. We were both just sitting there, feeding our babies. We could have been anywhere. I heard the noise of the children coming back. There was a terrific blast of air, the fire went out and she walked out carrying the baby with her dress trailing behind her. The old iron grate was empty.

What can I make of the experience? It was hot and I was still in that strange state after birth when you are not sure where you end and the baby starts. Did I want something very special to happen in a magical place with a very special new baby because I felt very close to all women who were mothers? Or did the babies link me with the other woman across the centuries? Perhaps it was not just a mental aberration on my part.

Some mothers feel that the link with their child begins even before birth. Jane, the health professional I mentioned earlier in the chapter, tells how a woman who had taken an anti-sickness drug in the early months of pregnancy, though not the one implicated in birth deformities, was convinced throughout that there was something wrong with her baby. There was absolutely no clinical evidence to suggest this and the medical professionals did their best to reassure her. But things were not right. When the baby was born, he had to be transferred to the special care unit where he died. Jane says: 'Perhaps we were too ready to say there was no evidence and so there was nothing wrong. Perhaps we should have listened to her and tried to pinpoint her anxieties. Maybe it was her sixth sense that told her something was wrong.'

She also reports another case where a couple were over the moon about the impending birth of their child and the pregnancy went very smoothly. But when the wife went into labour, the couple felt completely flat. The baby was born with a severe handicap and died a couple of days later. Jane says it was as if the flatness was like a cushion to ease them into the tragedy, because there was no apparent reason for them both to feel that way – when labour began everything seemed fine. Again it was as though a sixth sense was at work. She adds that a number of pregnant women who report that they do not feel pregnant, subsequently go on to miscarry – in each case the mother seemed to have picked up that all was not well.

Hazel says: 'My first son was born 13 years ago at 31 weeks. He was born at 10pm and I knew he was too early to have a strong chance of survival. He was taken to the special care baby unit, where I spent a couple of hours with him and my husband visited too. Then at 1am I woke up suddenly from sleep and had an urgent desire to see my baby. The night nurse phoned the special care unit and I was told the doctor would be coming up to talk to me. She came and told me my son had just died. I asked to see him. But the doctor was not happy about this. She said they had done their best to save him. I believe we do have this extra sense of communication with our young children.'

A baby may sometimes appear to be transmitting his or her feelings or moods to the mother from the womb. Wendy told me: 'When I was eight months pregnant I had gone to a party with my husband given by some of his work colleagues. The disco music was very loud, so I asked my husband to turn it down, not because it was bothering me but because there was a complete feeling of panic coming from my stomach. The baby wasn't kicking or punching, but I could feel his fear. It wasn't like a normal panic which comes from the head and the throat but was definitely seated in my stomach. After a while the noise level started creeping up again. In the end, I had to insist on leaving as I picked up what the baby was feeling and felt I had to protect him.'

Was the baby trying to communicate or were Wendy's worries about the child coming to the surface? Loud noises and anxiety in the mother do seem to increase the rate of the foetal heartbeat and frequency of foetal movement, which could convey to the mother the feeling that the baby was unhappy. But in Wendy's case, the baby wasn't moving and she is sure that she was not panicking.

Some people actually claim to have memories of their life in the womb. Mary recalls a brief moment before she was born – 'simply being contained within my mother and a sense of weariness which I shared with her, her weariness and her complete unawareness of me as a person'. Age may be playing tricks with Mary's memory or causing her to fantasise, but it is conceivable that these pre-birth experiences were felt so strongly that they have remained with her through life.

Rebirthers believe that many traumas or anxieties in later life can be traced to memories, conscious or unconscious, of our time in the womb and the actual birth process. Liz Cornish told me: 'The baby will pick up on everything that is going on with the mother while it is in the womb and pick up her traumas and neuroses.' She tells of a successful advertising executive who had terrible anxieties centred around money. It turned out that his father had been made bankrupt just before he was born and his mother was forced to take a cleaning job to make ends meet. Liz believes that Tim picked up his mother's anxieties about money before and just after his birth and has unconsciously been reacting to them ever since.

Conventional medical opinion acknowledges that a mother's psychological as well as physical well-being is important to the growing foetus, because of the physiological changes stress and other emotion bring to the body which are passed across the placenta to the growing child. And, as Janet Boucher, a child psychiatrist, points out, there is no reason to assume that memory is something that is not switched on before the moment of birth. Memory of the close emotional bond forged between a mother and the child in her womb could be carried into their relationship after birth, and this may be the clue to the apparently magical powers of communication that so often exist between mothers and their new-born infants.

4

Looking Ahead

It might seem wonderful to be able to foresee the future but it can have unpleasant side effects. Often the messenger gets the blame for bringing bad news as Pat found out.

'When I was thirteen,' she told me, 'it was the first time one of my dreams came true. I woke up and did not want my breakfast. "What's the matter with you?" mum asked in her usual brisk way. "I had an awful dream someone was at the bottom of the pool," I said, meaning the small lake in the town. Mum sent me off to school and told me not to be stupid. But when I got home the door was locked. It was never locked so I was worried. I knocked and mum opened it. I will never forget her words. "Your bloody dream," she said. Her cousin had drowned in the pool that day. Her sight was failing and she had mistaken the algae growing round the edge of the pool for grass and had walked on it. All this was 40 years ago, but I can still remember how terrified I was and how furious my mother was. "Your bloody dream," she kept saying.'

Even pleasant predictions can misfire. Dorothy, now a grandmother, can remember when she was twelve going to a dancing club with her mother. There she told a friend of her mother: 'You are going to win the raffle.' The prediction was correct but Dorothy found herself the target of a lot of anger because everyone thought the raffle had been fixed.

Joy, a correspondent from Mckinleyville in the United States, told me the story of her Aunt Florence who was born in Nebraska in 1887. 'Florence was at a sports day at her little school. They all sat in makeshift bleachers [raised stalls] to watch. Girls in those days were so prim and Victorian and Florence, being pretty, was especially afraid to call any attention to herself. In the middle of the game, Florence leapt up, shouted "Run" at the top of her little voice and dashed down the field. When she looked back, everyone was staring at her and she wanted to disappear into a hole. At that point the bleachers collapsed. Many children were hurt.' Florence may have been right to act as she did on this occasion but, wrote Joy, it brought her little happiness. 'This aunt of mine was a much misunderstood woman and had a sad life.'

Predictions need not always bring bad news but can sometimes herald a relatively minor event. Julie says that when her son was just starting to talk, at about nine o'clock one morning, he suddenly mentioned a Mrs Hansard. 'I was surprised because she was an old family friend whose name he would never have heard in his life. I had not spoken nor heard of her since I was a child. But that day, out of the blue, I got a letter from her.' Coincidence or something deeper? With the sometimes uncertain state of the mail it would be useful to have a child around the house who could accurately predict when letters were going to arrive – or even better, alert you when they got lost in the post.

Another Dorothy, who is a psychic artist and colour therapist, says that a predictive dream revealed the whereabouts of the grandfather she desperately wanted as a child. 'My one grandad died before I was born and my father's father was just not there. My father thought he was dead. One day when I was seven and a half, I got to my nan's house and the door was locked. I panicked because it was always open. She let us in and a gentleman was there. He gave my sister and I half a crown each for sweets and his ration book to take to the sweet shop. When we got back (we hadn't nearly been able to spend all that money on sweets – it was a fortune) Nan said: "Go down to the station and watch the trains while you are eating your sweets."

'When we got back from our feast, the man was gone. "Who was that?" I asked Nan. "Oh, that was your grandad," she said. So I did have a grandad like other children. But he was gone again. Then I started to dream about finding him. I used to see myself go out of the front door and through the garden and try all sorts of ways out of Nottingham until eventually I found grandad's house. It was on a very wide road that narrowed at the bottom, running down a very steep hill. There was a railway track that went under the road. I stopped at the junction and one way the road passed some trees. There was grandad living in a big house, being looked after by servants. I had that dream for several years.

'My grandmother died when I was twenty-five. In the

following May, my aunt contacted my father to say that she had discovered where grandad was. He had written to my grandmother sending money, but she had been in hospital for six months and her old house had been sold in that time. The old man had been in hospital himself and his address had changed. I arranged to go with my husband and children to see him the next day.

'We found ourselves in a very wide road, but I knew exactly where to go because it was all as in my dream – the railway going under the road, the trees and even the big house where my grandfather was living. In a sense, the dream was totally accurate because grandad was being looked after by "servants". They were care assistants. He was living in an old people's home.'

My research also revealed that children could apparently spark off premonitions as well as have them. Of Maureen's four children, Colin, the youngest was the only one still at school and living at home. 'We were a loving, close-knit family, very talkative and enjoying each other's company. One night I had a dream. I dreamt that Colin was dead. I was standing in the kitchen, very distressed and was saying: "Colin's dead and Myra [a friend of the family] doesn't even know." There seemed to be no body around and I didn't see the scene of death. He just wasn't there. When I first got up out of bed I didn't even think of it. It came back to me as dreams do when Colin was ready to leave to catch the school bus. I was standing by the kitchen sink and he came up and said: "I'm going now, mum." I replied, "Oh, Colin, I dreamt you were dead." I looked at him and he put his arms round me. I hugged him close. He laughed and I kissed him out of sheer joy and love. He smiled his gentle, smirky smile that he always gave when he was pleased, when I said I was so glad he wasn't dead. This wasn't our usual morning farewell as we mostly were in a tearing rush to get out. I followed him to the door and he laughed as he went off to catch his bus. Colin's father, who had retired early, always stayed in bed until the family rush was over, but that day he had got up specially to watch Colin walk to the bus stop, thinking to himself what a fine lad his son was.

'Colin had little to do at school that afternoon and he must have come home early but just missed us – his father, grandmother and I had gone out for a short drive. He probably came home, found the door locked (he had left his key in his bedroom) and went for a walk down a nearby lane which leads to 200 foot high cliffs. He was not seen again for two days.

'During that time,' wrote Maureen, 'there were some odd occurences. The following morning my mother was about to get up and was half awake so she could have been dreaming, but she thought she saw Colin in a corner of the bedroom. He was leaning against a wall or rock with his coat half over his shoulder and his right eye cut and blood running down the side of his face. My mother said she put out her arms to him and said, "Colin, Colin, is that you Colin?" but he just faded away.

'During the day I had a strong desire to go and look along the shore – though there was no more reason why he should have gone there than anywhere else. The weather was atrocious. It was the wettest two days for many years and there was a thick dark mist. By tea-time, I felt so impelled to walk down the lane to the cliffs, where there was an old mine shaft, I ploughed through the mist and on reaching the mine-shaft, called for Colin. I didn't know then that he lay on the rocks below me. His body was found there two days later.

'The following Tuesday, I was getting tea ready in the kitchen, when I had the oddest sensation again. My friend Myra – the Myra of the dream – was due home from her holiday abroad. She had not been told the bad news. I suddenly realised she was due home that day and said: "Myra is coming home today and she doesn't know that Colin is dead." It was like a replay of the dream.

'The evening before the funeral, my family arrived. There were 14 of us. I decided it would be best if I slept in Colin's bed. Such a feeling of love and peace I have never experienced either before or since. I felt cocooned in absolute peace as I lay in Colin's bed. I slept like a log and woke the next morning still feeling the same.

'My eldest son told me I was just seeing into things what I wanted – perhaps he is right. I don't know but I sometimes feel as if all these incidents were a glimmer of something sent to comfort us or perhaps we subconsciously know the pattern of our lives. It seems strange that of all our family this should happen to Colin. He was the one who was always afraid to go near the edges of cliffs.'

Just after the last world war, Cathy also had a premonition that her child was going to die. 'When my little boy was ill in hospital many years ago, I was cooking some potatoes in a pan. Suddenly the boiling water cleared and I could see church writing written on the water – "In the midst of life, we are in death". I was very upset and dashed to the hospital. The porter was surprised to see me as he had only just put the phone down to summon me to come to the hospital as my little boy was getting worse. We lost him that night. But those words in the pan I think helped me to cushion the shock of losing him as he was only two.'

In both the previous two cases, the mothers saw their premonitions as something which prepared them for disaster and thereby softened the blow. They also felt that death was not just blind fate, but part of a pre-ordained pattern. Sceptics could say that Cathy's vision may well have been brought on by worry, as her child was already very ill. Also, it could be argued that Maureen's dream expressed a mother's fears about her son growing up and moving away from her. But Maureen's dream was so vivid and accurate and made some sense of a tragedy that would otherwise have seemed just pointless. Any attempt to push for a logical explanation would trivialise what was for Maureen a very special farewell.

Quite often a premonition consists only of a strong feeling or compulsion to do something. Marian wrote from Ireland: 'I was sewing in school when I suddenly dropped the sewing. I got a terrible urge to go home. My father was very ill at home at the time and the ambulance was due to call for him at 5pm as he was going to hospital in Dublin. Our teacher asked me what was wrong. I told her I had to go home and I could not even wait to get permission from the Reverend Mother. I even left my school bag behind so I could run faster. When I ran in the front door my mother said: "How did you know?" It seems they had got word that the ambulance had to come earlier than expected and so I was there to see him off. I had a terrible feeling that he would never be back, even though I hadn't been told at the time that he had cancer. I never saw my father again.'

Ellie too had many premonitions which came either as strong feeling or sometimes as pictures in her mind. When I met her she was fourteen and told me: 'When I was about ten, I was sat watching the television when my mind went blank and I thought to myself, "If my father has had an accident I shall take a small bunch of grapes with a huge red ribbon tied to them to him in hospital." About five minutes later there was a phone call from my mother, who was crying, to tell me that dad had had an accident and was in hospital.

'Then a few weeks ago I was constantly thinking about a family we knew in America. In all my lessons I sat and thought about them and their boat, where they lived and their way of life. Soon after we received a phone call telling us they had been in a car crash. The husband and child were both dead but the wife had survived. Thinking about this has made me realise that most things that happen out of the ordinary are to do with people close to you. Because of this we are aware of them even when we are far away and can sometimes predict their thoughts and even their actions.'

Many premonitions, however, do seem to come in the form of a dream. Timothy, who attends a boarding school, regularly has predictive dreams. 'A couple of weeks ago I had a dream that Anne, our next door but one neighbour, was going to fall ill or something was going to happen to her. I kept it to myself until I went home and my mother told me she had had a heart attack. She survived and is now out of hospital.' Had he noticed something about his next door neighbour without realising it, that made him concerned for her health? Or did he have 'the sight' in a moment of stress?

Michelle's dream, which predicted an accident for her uncle when she was a young teenager, was powerful enough to return three times. She wrote: 'He was covered to the chin with a white sheet. He was very ill. I said, "What's the matter Uncle John?" but he could not tell me. The following night I had the dream again. I asked him if he had been in an accident but he could not answer and I woke up screaming. The third night I had the dream again. I told my mum the next morning. A month later at 5.30am I woke up with a terrific pain in my head. I fell back to sleep but an hour and a half later my mum woke me to say Uncle John had been in a car accident about an hour before. She went to see him in hospital. He was covered up to the chin with a massive white sheet – just as in my dream.'

Memories of predictive dreams which have come true can be so vivid that they stay with you over the years. In 1932 Ronald was in his first year at secondary school. He shared art lessons with boys from other forms and greatly admired a boy called Peter, though he was too shy to speak to him. 'During the long summer holiday, I dreamt that I attended Peter's funeral. I could see the coffin being lowered into the grave, though I had never attended a funeral, so far as I can recollect. The impression was so vivid that I can still see it all now as I write and as soon as school recommenced after the holiday, I asked after Peter of a formmate whom I knew lived near him. He told me that Peter had died from diptheria during the school holiday.'

Ruth, aged twelve, has had only one predictive dream which she does not really like to remember. 'I saw a clock which said 7.15. It was very dark and then I was in my friend's room which was black. In the dream, she had died of leukaemia in hospital. Three weeks later my friend died in hospital. When I asked what time they said 7.15pm. She was asleep when she died and I thought that would account for the dark room in my dream.' Ruth was away at boarding school for a lot of the year and although she knew her friend was ill she had not known it was leukaemia, though she may have sensed how ill her friend was and subconsciously guessed what was wrong. However, her dream did seem to mirror her friend's death. Ruth did not want to talk about it any more.

James' mother did not take him seriously when he told her he had dreamt about a disaster involving a big boat. 'I had a dream about a big boat that left the harbour, then went half way out and then crash and was lying on its side. In the morning, I told my mum and she said, "Don't worry, you can dream about all sorts of things," and pulled my leg about it. I was really worried and wondered if I ought to phone the police, but I thought they would think it was a stunt or I was a crank. Then two days later there was the Zeebrugge disaster.'

Dreams about disasters are common and there are some well documented cases involving children. In April 1912, a young girl in Nottingham told her grandmother about a dream in which a large boat sank in the local park. The next day news broke of the sinking of the Titanic. The girls' uncle was among the dead.

After the Aberfan disaster in 1966 when part of a giant coal tip slid down on to a village school in South Wales, killing 128 children and 16 adults, Dr J. C. Barker* made a nationwide appeal for premonitions about the tragedy. One of the few accurate predictions and certainly the saddest came from the parents of a ten-year-old victim. Shortly before the disaster, she had told her mother that she had dreamt she had gone to school and there was no school there. Something black had come down all over it. But a problem with that study was that it asked about a past event. It is easy to say, 'Oh I knew that was going to happen,' afterwards. A premonition can only really be regarded as believable, if it is reported in advance of the event it predicts. As a long-term project I have begun a prediction bureau, asking children to send me accounts of dreams or premonitions they feel certain could come true. Then if anything does happen as the child predicts, I will be able to verify that it was forecast with foresight and not with hindsight.

It is, as I have said, a long-term project which has not yet borne fruit. But while waiting, it does raise interesting speculation about what would happen if it was conclusively proved that some young people could predict the future with accuracy. Would it be possible to take them and train them as prophets and how could you guard against children with such a priceless gift being exploited, either by greedy individuals or the state? Then even if we could isolate and develop this ability (which would turn current scientific theories about time on their head), there is no guarantee that all the gifted children we discovered would be willing to increase any power they might have.

*An account of this is given in Dr Barker's book, *Scared to Death*, Frederick Muller, 1968.

May's young daughter is troubled by her predictive ability, which she has had from a very early age. Once she woke up afraid and weeping and said, 'If we get through Friday we'll be all right.' 'We did get through Friday,' said May. 'Then I heard that a dear friend travelling in the USA had had a serious injury on that Friday and had to be flown home for surgery. My daughter often seems to know who is going to phone fifteen minutes before they do. She will say, "Don't get the coffee yet. Esther is going to ring you." There is usually no special time that the people concerned normally ring, so it is really strange. My daughter doesn't like being able to do this and is not keen to develop it.'

5

Ghosts and Phantom Voices

'We used to have ghosts ages ago but not any more,' said John aged six. This was typical of the type of answer I got when I asked very young children whether they had ever seen a ghost. But I was not totally surprised by these replies. I had expected little or no information from such young children about any psychic experiences, because at their age they see little difference between the natural and the supernatural. Jack's clairvoyance, that I mentioned in Chapter 1, was of no importance to him personally although it shook us. He is still far more excited by something like a large empty cardboard box which his imagination can transform into a space ship or a castle. But it must be frustrating for psychic researchers who are trying to get children to co-operate. As one respected investigator put it: 'I agree children can be a fruitful field of study but because of the hassle involved it's often just not worth it.'

As it turned out my first ghost story came to me completely by chance. I had been telling Rosemary, a friend, about Jack's experiences over coffee when she said: 'My friend's son saw his great-grandmother's ghost at her funeral.' This set the pattern for the following months, as little by little I began to meet people and hear their stories. Like Rosemary's friend, Veronica, they were nearly always perfectly ordinary people to whom something had happened for which they could find no rational explanation and therefore they were wary of broadcasting it to a disbelieving world.

Matthew, Veronica's son, had had a real bond with his great-grandmother and in many ways was closer to her than anyone else. He is an only child, very bright and very articulate. Veronica told me that when Matthew was about two, he used to be taken every Saturday to an old people's home to see his great-grandmother, who was suffering from progressive senile dementia. She eventually became incapable of speech and her eyesight became very poor. Towards the end the only person she would respond to was Matthew. Veronica and her husband would place him in front of the old lady. Then Matthew's dad would tap on the metal tray beside her bed to attract her attention. It was a routine they had. She knew then that Matthew was there and would run her fingers over his face, smiling and trying to make noises.

Veronica says that Matthew treated her as if she was another child. He called her his 'little great-nanny' as she had shrunk to around four foot in height and was very frail. When she died, Matthew was not quite three. He was taken to her funeral because he did not take well to being left with other people and Veronica was confident he would not be upset. 'Matthew had his head lifted towards the crematorium ceiling which was totally plain,' said Veronica. 'As the coffin came along, he started to say he could see his great-nanna on the ceiling. "Look there's little great-nanny. She's smiling," he kept saying looking upwards. He carried on saying this until the curtains closed around the coffin when he said, "Look, she's gone now." There was no mistaking what Matthew said because he was so articulate.

'Matthew saw his "little great-nanny" a couple of times in his bedroom over the next couple of months, though not on the night of the funeral. He would say nanna or little great-nanny is smiling. He wasn't at all frightened. He is now six and he hasn't mentioned seeing her since.'

Young children will try to make sense of death in terms of their limited experience and vivid imaginations. Had Matthew overheard some adult saying 'She's gone above' and used that to try to make sense of why his great-grandmother had disappeared? Did he think that as he could not go to see nanna any more, she might come to him. Children do work hard at making sense of death, but Professor George Wall, a professor of philosophy at Lamar University in Texas, thinks that psychological explanations are not always adequate for children's psychic experiences. In Matthew's case, it is hard to explain the crematorium incident away. Perhaps his great-grandmother did continue to smile at the only person she had communicated with to the end, the only person who could still make her smile.

Grandad Bert was not the most popular member of his family and had few friends, so perhaps he thought he had better alert everyone that he had passed over or attendance would be a bit thin on the ground at his funeral.

His lack of popularity may also be why he chose to appear to the youngest member of the family, whom he might have thought would give him the most enthusiastic reception. It was left to his young great-grandaughter, who was barely two-years-old at the time, to alert her family to his demise. Carla, the little girl's mother, told me that she and the children hardly ever saw grandad Bert. He was an overbearing man at the best of times and when he developed senile dementia, he became so problematic that Carla felt she could not face taking the children to see him.

He died unexpectedly at about 4am on a Wednesday morning, but since the family had lost touch, Carla was not told. She said: 'At about 11 o'clock that morning, my little girl, Layla, stopped playing in the living room and looked up as if she was looking into someone's face. "It's grandad Bert," she said and ran to where, apparently, he was standing and looked up into his face. Then she shrugged as if to say, "Oh he's gone", and ran back and carried on playing. I thought this was odd, especially as we never saw grandad Bert. So when my husband came home at about 4 o'clock in the afternoon I said: "I suppose we'd better see if he's all right." So he rang his mum and she said that grandad Bert had died early that morning.'

Uncle Fred's spirit went round the world to bring news of his departure to distant relatives. Mandy, then a young teenager was living in Perth, Australia when her great-uncle died in England. He had been ill for a relatively short time and Mandy's family had not been told about it. But when Mandy's aunt rang to tell them her husband had died, Mandy's father was not surprised by the news.

The previous night, Uncle Fred had appeared to Mandy at the end of her bed and she had rushed into her parents' room crying: 'Uncle Fred's dead. I saw him.' However, Mandy had never met Uncle Fred and had seen no recent photographs of him. Yet she recognised him instantly.

The story of the apparition caused some trouble in the family as Fred had a daughter, about the same age as Mandy, who had helped to nurse him. She and her sisters were upset that he had not appeared to them, but to a comparative stranger halfway around the world.

In Julie's case, she wasn't the only person to see her late uncle. Aunty Doris, his widow, chatted to him regularly and was therefore regarded as being a bit dotty by the rest of the family. When she was five or six, Julie would go on family visits to Aunty Doris, which were regarded as a bit of a chore. 'When we went round, there she was chatting away to her dead husband. They all thought she was "off her trolley", but I could see him as well. Aunty once took me into her bedroom to give me a sweet and said: "You don't think I'm dotty, do you? You can see him too, can't you?" I had never met him in real life, but from pictures, I realised it was him I saw. I did not say anything about it to anybody. I don't know why.'

Thomas told the story of his mother who when a young girl met her grandmother's ghost in the street. 'She was walking with her four sisters when she saw gran coming towards them and stepped off the footpath to let her pass by. Gran did not speak and seemed to be wrapped up in her thoughts. Mum's sister said, "What did you do that for – there's no one there?" Mum didn't reply. She told me she saw her grandmother complete with poke bonnet and shawl, but her sisters had obviously seen nothing.

When they got home, their mother told them that gran had just died.'

But a prize for the most unconventional return would have to go to Jane's grandmother, who apparently performed an act of supernatural ventriloquism. When Jane's daughter was four, the family were staying in Aberdeen for a christening. 'The eldest child of the family we were staying with was being a real pain, so I took him and my daughter to the local park. We were playing in the bandstand in the twilight, dancing round to *Ring-a-Ring-a-Roses* and we got to a bit I didn't know about "fishes in the water, fishes in the sea". We were skipping round when my daughter's voice changed and she was singing in the voice of my much-loved paternal grandmother who had been dead for twelve years. She had her funny accent – a Welsh one – and was emphasising the words exactly as nan used to. I expected to see my nan there. It was a very happy experience.'

Sally also told me about a phantom voice, that of her father, which she kept hearing for the first four months after he died when she was twelve. 'It was typical of him,' she said. 'He came in the door and shouted, "Ooo-ooh", just as he used to when he was alive. Once mum and I heard him at the same time. I was upstairs and I heard him call downstairs and she was downstairs and heard him calling upstairs. I once heard him when I was taking the dog out for a walk. Another time, I was sitting at the dining room table doing my homework, when I looked up and there he was on the stairs holding the banister. He was wearing clothes I recognised, but as I looked at his face he vanished. I wasn't scared, it was nice, I just thought, "It's dad but it can't be." I never saw him again after that, but I used to feel him around.'

It should be obvious by now that ghosts very often appear to people they are related to, even if they never knew those people in life. One of the most interesting stories I heard came from Sheila, whose grandson, Darren, was born about five months after his father, Kevin, died in a car accident. Darren is now eleven and, although he never knew his father, follows his dad in every way – the same looks, the same mannerisms and the same love of football. 'He walks like his dad, talks like his dad and writes like his dad,' says Sheila. However, he has been brought up in an area well away from his former home, as his grief-stricken mother, who was widowed at twenty-one, couldn't bear too many reminders of Kevin. But, according to Sheila, Kevin has been part of Darren's life since he was very young. Sheila remembers: 'When Darren was only two-and-a-half, we were living in a country cottage and he and his mum were staying with us. Suddenly he pointed over to a chair and said, "Look, mummy, there's the nice daddy man." He was pointing to Kevin's special chair. "Where? What are you talking about?" Debbie asked. "It's the daddy man in our picture," Darren explained. "Oh, he's gone now."'

Then when Darren was three, Sheila got out some old photos to amuse him. 'One showed Kevin with a group of friends when he was eight. It was so long ago that I didn't immediately recognise which one was my son,' she told me, 'but Darren identified his father straight away. "Look Nan," he cried, "boy Kevin, boy daddy." His mum was very upset by the incident and said, "Not that again! He keeps on and on that he sees his daddy and talks to him."'

Later when Darren was about six, Sheila says he told

her: 'I see my daddy Kevin. I know my daddy Kevin. I love my daddy Kevin, but it is so difficult to talk to grown-ups about it. But you know, nanny, you understand.' He was staying with Sheila at the time. 'I look after old people and Darren used to love visiting them. One old lady was quite badly handicapped, but was always very cheerful. One particular day she was crying and told Darren that her friend she had known for thirty years had just died. "Don't cry," he said. "Your friend is with Jesus." Then he paused thoughtfully and continued, "No, that's what they tell me, that my daddy is with Jesus, but he's not. He is with me. I see my daddy Kevin and I know him. He talks to me and he comes to me when I am in trouble. I say come on daddy Kevin, put it right and he does." Kevin at eleven still tells me that he sometimes sees and talks to his father, though he loves his stepfather and his new brother very much and is very happy in his new life. But "daddy Kevin" is still there for him.'

When ghosts are not related at all to the people who see them, there is often a strong emotional link. In the case of Genevie who lived near San Diego, California, it was the child who was the ghost. Genevie's cousin Joy told me the story: 'Genevie was substitute teaching in a school near San Diego in the 1970s. One little boy in her class was very sensitive, abysmally poor and very much in need of attention. He was Mexican. Genevie liked him very much and did what she could for him. One Saturday, as she was driving along the main road, the little boy jumped smiling right in front of her car. She was so start-led she swerved and had to stop and sit at the road side recovering for a second or two. But when she got out of the car, she couldn't see the little boy anywhere. The boy's family had no phone and doubled up in a shack someplace, so she couldn't find out if he was all right until school on Monday morning. Then she received notice that he had drowned at the very moment she saw him. She feels he somehow came to say goodbye to her.'

It is probably a lot easier to see ghosts if you live in a big manor house with portraits round the walls. Then mum may well encourage the belief in ghosts. But for ordinary children from ordinary homes, ghosts are a bit more of a problem. Especially at school where it can be awkward to be different. Sue, who is convinced she shared her life with fairies and people from another world as a child (see also Chapters 7 and 12), once said to a schoolfriend: 'I expect you see what I see?' She was rapidly disillusioned and very quickly learnt to keep quiet. Dorothy, a psychic artist, clairvoyant and healer, had similar problems. She was always drawing faces as a child of the phantoms she says she could see around her. Her schoolfriends would ask who she was drawing and at first she would say: 'It's somebody I can see.' But they would look round and laugh, so she quickly learnt to keep quiet about what she saw and say, when they asked who she was drawing, 'Well, it can be anybody you like.'

Patricia told me that when she was ten, she saw the ghost of a woman with a big shawl, a Spanish comb in her hair and lots of rings on her fingers. She was about 75. 'I was very scared when I saw her and she vanished when I spoke. I told mum, but she told me not to be silly and to go back to bed. I had six brothers and sisters and was told I musn't frighten them.' But later, when Patricia was listening on the stairs, she overheard her mum say to her dad, 'Pat's just seen Old Mother Moore.' This was a woman who had died while living in the shop which Patricia's parents had taken over.

Wendy's ghosts weren't even the conventional 'lady in grey' type, though in their own way they were just as exotic. 'When I was about four,' she told me, 'I woke up to see two figures at the end of my bed. They were two men dressed as boxers, with long boxing shorts. They were full-sized. We were living in Derby at the time, by the prison, and there was an old army blanket across the window to dim the light from the street lamp, but I could see both figures very clearly and was unafraid. I was quite awake and very curious. I didn't mention the incident to my parents. I didn't want to be told off for being silly. But I did tell another child who used to walk with me home from school. She told me very firmly that there were no ghosts but the Holy Ghost. I think I made an early decision that God's disapproval was too much of a risk and I don't remember ever seeing another ghost after that.'

As a child, Jane, now in her thirties, twice saw people no one else could see. The first time was when she was 10 or 11 and attending a school swimming gala at an old Edwardian baths. Throughout the proceedings, she says that a strange little girl kept coming in and out of the gallery opposite, carrying a little wooden sword, and wearing a pinny with a red cross on it and strange clothes made of crepe paper. 'I found it most distracting. Yet no one else seemed to notice. Afterwards when I asked, I realised I was the only person to see her. Then not long after I was on a school visit to London and passed this big old house. It was a white building and the garden was absolutely filled with people in old-style peasant costume, picking fruit off the trees. When I asked, discreetly, no one else had seen anything. When I went past the house years later, the garden was very small, nothing like the orchard I had seen.'

In all the cases I have just mentioned, the children were very nervous of talking about their experiences in case they were laughed at or rebuked, but in Beverley's case, her mother also saw the ghosts, though it was not till many years later that she admitted it. Beverley remembers: 'I woke in the middle of the night to find several human figures floating past the bed. The figures were like sharp shadows, black in silhouette, but not against a wall – rather like black cardboard cut-outs in profile. There were several, but I was most aware of a portly gentleman who passed by. His image was so sharp that I can recall the outline of his waistcoat buttons and cutaway coat. As they went out of the door, I seemed to lose sight of them. I called out to my mother who came into the room. At the time, she said she couldn't see anything but later admitted that she could and told me she hadn't wanted to frighten me. I remember telling her: "One's just gone right through you."'

Beverley's mother, Joy, also recalls the incident and confirmed that her motive for telling Beverley at the time that she was dreaming was that she did not want to worry her. 'I remember it very clearly. I wish I had written the date down in my diary but at the time was more anxious to gloss the incident over, although strangely it wasn't at all frightening. But I thought at the time, Beverley might have been worried. On this particular night, she called out and I got out of bed and went to her bedroom which was next to ours. On reaching the door, which was slightly open, I was startled to see this group of figures standing just inside the door. It was a small group of dark figures, very plain but the faces were not clear. Beverley was sitting up in bed and said, "Can't you see them?" I tried to dismiss the incident and said, "You must be dreaming." Then I moved forward and suddenly the figures glided towards the end of the room and disappeared. One figure was noticeably shorter than the others and they appeared to be wearing cloaks and had tall hats which led us to believe later that they might be Quakers, especially as we lived near a historic Quaker area. We did not, of course, discuss all this at the time. Afterwards, I wondered if there had been a path or something through the room at one time. Beverley shared the room with her older sister who slept through the whole incident, but who had said on several occasions that she had been compelled to run upstairs because she thought there was someone behind her.'

One of the problems of adult recollections of childhood is that adults are adept at reading something back into their childhood experiences and tend to give an account tinged by what they know now. But while many memories are changed by subsequent experience, particularly vivid or startling episodes are frequently preserved intact. Non-psychic examples of this are the 'flashbulb' memories that seem to take in the surrounding context. People can often remember precisely what they were doing the day John Kennedy was assassinated or when a man first walked on the moon. They can recall the music they were listening to, what they were wearing and who they were with – even such trivial details seem to be permanently etched in the memory.

Madame Robert is now seventy and lives in Brittany in

a home full of treasures from Pondicherry, the French en-
clave in India where she and her sister were brought up
before the Second World War. Her sister, Denise,
appears to have been highly sensitive to psychic phenomena and Madame Robert can clearly remember a number of incidents that caused quite a stir in their family at
the time. Their father held an important post in the dis-
trict and often the village headman would come to see
him in his garden to discuss business. Denise was eight
when she said to her father one evening, 'There's the old
head of the village who has a hole in his ear. He's come
and says he wants to see you.' 'We searched everywhere,'
recalled Madame Robert, 'but there was no one. The next
day, the son of the village headman came in the morning
and announced to my father that the chief had died the
previous evening – at the time Denise had said she had
seen him.'

Later the family moved to a property on the outskirts
of Pondicherry. It was near a lake and dated back to 1800.
One evening, she, her mother and sister were having a
moonlight picnic by the lake, when suddenly Denise said,
'I can see something beside the tree. It's a woman all
clothed in white who is holding something in her hands
and is crying. Behind her is a man dressed in a large
checked cape and he has a beard.' Madame Robert and
her mother couldn't see anything, but Denise walked up
to the woman and asked her her name. 'My sister asked
several times and then came back and told us that the
woman was called Theresa. We did not find out why she
was crying.

'The next day we went to see the man who sold us the
property and asked if he still had the documents from the

time the house was built. He produced a huge packet of documents and we found out that the house had once belonged to a Madame Theresa de Colomb.

'My sister often saw the lady in white but we could never learn why she was crying. Eventually, because it was not considered healthy to cohabit with phantoms, we asked a priest to purify the house and garden and this was done. Some time later two other people, who learnt we had bought the property, told us of visions they had had on past visits there. One spoke of the woman in white who cried and the other also mentioned the man with the beard and checked cape. However, we did not talk about Denise's visions.'

The real problem, however, in researching children's experiences of seeing ghosts, is being sure what it is a child is actually describing. Young children's language can be very vivid, but nevertheless, misleading. Last year we were camping in the New Forest when Jack came dashing into the tent and announced, 'Quick, mummy, there's an enormous panda bear outside.' Knowing we were less than ten miles from Marwell Zoo Park, my first reaction was to panic and warn all and sundry that there was a wild animal on the loose. My second instinct was to assume it was either a flight of Jack's fantasy world or his psychic powers were at work again and this time he had seen a ghost!

Both reactions would have been wrong. When I looked out of the tent the panda turned out to be a large black and white cow, with a face marked just like the panda in the story book Jack had just been looking at. Jack had neither lied nor fantasised but had described what he saw in terms of a recent experience that was still fresh in his memory. So the next time your child tells you that he's seen something strange, have a look. He might be playing you up or, like Jack, he might have got it completely wrong, but on the other hand . . .

6

Lives Cut Short

The most harrowing ghost stories I was told in the course
of my research were those about the ghosts of children.
Too often psychic investigators forget that ghosts were
once real flesh and blood people who lived and loved and
were loved in return. When a child dies the death leaves a
permanent scar on the souls of its parents. As Janet
Boucher put it, although the mother may be physically
separated from the baby when it is born, the links remain
and when the child dies, emotionally a bit of the parent
dies too.

When a handicapped child dies, the grief is not only for
the child who died but also for the child who never was.
Jackie who died when she was twelve had never been able
to speak or walk. Her mother told how her daughter died
after a year in hospital and during that time the family
had moved house, so Jackie never got to see her new
home. 'As I stood in the kitchen after the funeral with my
friends and family all around, above the chattering, I

heard a voice. It said: "Don't worry about me, mummy. I am all right now." Jackie had never been able to speak, so she had never even said mummy. I have since wondered if I had always wanted to hear that. On the other hand, I am sure I would have never expected her to talk.

'Jackie died before Christmas. On New Years' Eve, some friends came to stay the night with their young son who was about two-and-a-half-years old. He slept with our three-year-old son in his room. Some months later, my friend told me what her son had said the following morning. She hadn't told me at the time for fear of upsetting me so soon after Jackie's death. He had asked her who the little girl was who had walked across the landing and looked into his bedroom. "You mean Christine [Jackie's younger sister]," his mother had said. But the little boy had replied, "No, this little girl had white [blonde] curly hair." He had described Jackie, whom he had not seen since he was nine months old. Jackie couldn't walk either, even with help.'

Richard is a farmer in New Zealand. I met him when he was visiting family in England. Sitting in the garden of a friend's house on a hot summer's day while his adopted son played with my children, he told me how an apparition had helped him come to terms with two tragedies.

His second son died when he was just a few days old at a time when the family were living in Rhodesia before it became Zimbabwe. The sanctions imposed against the country during the struggle for independence meant that Richard could not get the drugs to save the baby whose lungs were not fully developed. Eleven years later, in New Zealand, Joseph, Richard's eldest son died. 'We had only known for about ten days that there was something wrong with him,' he said, 'though no one knew what. Joseph had spasms during which he appeared to have difficulty breathing. We thought he was just exhausted, the problem would pass and he would be fine again. But on one occasion, the problem didn't pass and we took him to see a lady doctor who thought he was having asthma attacks.

'Joseph got up one morning, late for him as he had been reading late in bed the night before. He came into the sitting room and I gave him some tea. I always made tea for the children when they got up. Joseph said he was not feeling well. "Where are you feeling ill?" I asked him – he had not been able to explain what was wrong before – and for the first time, he pointed to his throat. Then he started to have spasms and lose control of his arms. I thought he was having an asthma attack. I called my wife to phone the doctor and I brought him to the table, sat him down and put him in the position the doctor had shown me. "I'm going to die, dad," he said. I held his shoulders and the tops of his arms. He threw his arms and head back and went mauve. He was unable to breathe. I put him on the ground and began mouth-to-mouth resuscitation.

'I continued until a nurse arrived about 20 minutes later. The lady doctor arrived about 30 minutes after that. After the best part of an hour, she said, "We have to stop now. There is no hope of reviving him." When the autopsy was carried out, it was discovered he was suffering from a very rare form of throat cancer that had developed only within the previous three months. There had only been 17 cases of it in medical history in the whole of New Zealand. How on earth could it happen to my boy? Two days before he died, Joseph had sat on my lap. I had put my arms around him and he had said, "You're the best dad in the world I could have had." Looking back, it was almost as if he was saying that he had experienced his life and knew he was going to die.'

Three years after Joseph's death, Richard was by himself in church on a Saturday evening after attending mass. 'I saw the two boys, but they were not the ages they were when they died. They were both in their teens, the ages they would have been if they had lived. They were both wearing the uniform of a Catholic college in Wellington. Joseph, for reasons of his own, had great ambitions to attend the school when he was old enough. They were kneeling beside me. Nothing was said. It was extraordinary and affirmed to me that death is a mere episode with no final division. The spirit had continued to go on through the days for those boys.'

Michael Jackson, the psychologist I mentioned in Chapter 1 who works at the Alister Hardy Research Centre in Oxford, says that Richard's experience of seeing his sons at the age they would be if they had lived is not at all unusual. He has observed in a number of accounts that when people lose a child and then see the child's ghost several years later, he or she will often have aged by the correct number of years. This is a phenomenon also experienced by May, who says her flat is haunted by the ghost of a little girl. 'She was very small when we first moved in but is now about eleven or twelve. She is dressed in an old fashioned pinafore with frills on it, white socks – long ones with buttons and has long blonde hair dressed in ringlets. She is very pretty. She does not speak but just comes into the room and stares at the wall. I just see her, then she goes.' Though May's present house is comparatively modern, it was built on a bomb site and there are still some very old houses in the area. 'I often wonder if the little girl lived in the house previously on this site,' she says.

A few months after meeting Richard, by lucky chance I met his wife Helen, during her short trip to England. Unlike her husband, she had not seen the ghost of her son Joseph, but she had heard from him. Not long after his death his best friend, Daniel, a boy of the same age, came to see her. 'I hope you don't mind me coming,' he said, 'but I saw Joe last night. Well, I didn't actually see him but I sort of felt him and I sort of heard him. I knew it was him because of his gravelly voice.' Helen told me that everyone thought Joe's voice was breaking. They did not relaise that the harsh quality was one of the effects of his throat cancer.

Daniel then told her what Joseph had said to him: '"Hello Dan," he said. "Oh Hello, Joe," I said. "What do you want?" "Would you do something for me Dan?" "Yes Joe, what is it?" "Would you go and see mum for me?" "Yes Joe. What do you want me to tell her?" "Nothing. I just wanted you to see if she was all right."'

The second message came about six months later from her friend Harriet who was always looking for something different to try. She was not particularly attracted to spiritualism or anything similar, said Helen, but when she saw a spiritualist meeting advertised in the local paper she thought it would be an interesting new experience and decided to go along. Harriet was bored stiff during the seance until suddenly the medium said, 'I've got a twelve-year-old boy here.' He clutched his throat. 'The boy died from throat cancer,' he said. 'The boy's mother is not here but her friend is,' and he came and stood by Harriet. 'Can you give his mother a message and tell her it's time she stopped grieving.' Helen says the contact was comforting and soothing and wonderful.

It may be that the ghosts of children find contact and comfort in the spiritual world. Peter King of the Reading National Spiritualist Church says that when children die, already dead grandparents or other relatives will often greet them and look after them on the other side. Annette, an American, lost her four-year-old son during the Second World War. 'A month after he died, I was ill in bed with chest pains and I had a dream. My mother who had died some years before was standing at the door. I hugged her and said, "What are you doing here?" "I've come because I had to see you," she replied. We went through into the kitchen and she picked up some bread and put it in the toaster. When it was ready, she buttered it and went to give it to me. "No," I said, "give it to the baby." My little boy was sitting in his high chair, looking very happy. "Now that's what I came for," said my mother. "Stop worrying about him. He's being well taken care of. He's a lovely little boy." When I woke up, the sun was streaming on my bed and my chest pains were gone.'

Flora's grand-daughter died when she was a year old. 'I just couldn't believe she had gone and I wouldn't settle down at night without thinking about her. I used to cry every night thinking about her because she was such a wonderful baby, though she must have been in a lot of pain. Then one night I felt a strange sensation and all of a sudden I was watching over my little grand-daughter. She was happy and was being looked after by my own mother. After seeing the baby so happy and out of pain, it really helped me. I told my daughter, who was the baby's mother, and it helped her too. My grand-daughter was a Down's syndrome baby, but was beautiful and gave plenty of love when she was with us.'

But what happens if the dead child is not greeted by people he knows on the other side? John, a father of three who works for an airline, believes that sometimes drumming it into children's minds that they should not go off with strangers can have unexpected results. For if a ghost child cannot find a friend he recognises in the afterlife, he may try to return to his still-alive family. And if they are not there, then the other thing he has been taught to do is to go to the people over the road he has known all his short life. John believes this is what happened to Paul, a neighbour's ten-year-old son, who was playing in a tin hut on a building site which caught fire. Paul suffered horrific burns and died in hospital five days later. Paul's mother, distraught with grief, moved out of her flat and refused to return to the area. 'My wife was so upset when she heard the news of Paul's death that she shut herself in the bathroom,' John told me. Then a few days later, 'I was downstairs when suddenly Paul walked in through the front door but turned his back on me.'

'Weren't you upset when you saw Paul?' I asked. John said he simply reacted like a father would have done. 'Well I couldn't bear the thought of him wandering around with no one to talk to, so I said, "Paul, won't you talk to me?" I couldn't see his face but I recognised his clothes. When I told his mum about all this later she said they were the ones he had worn on the day of the fire. Then I heard someone call his name. "Paul," I said, "you know you're always welcome here, but I think some other people are calling you and want you to go with them. I know you've been told not to go with people you don't know but you must go with these people." I couldn't see anyone else but I knew they were there. Then he was gone.

'I didn't immediately say anything about seeing Paul because I didn't want to upset my family. But when my daughter, who was only four, woke up I heard her call my eldest boy, who is Paul's age. "Alec, I saw Paul last night," she told her brother. Alec had been very close to Paul and was very upset by his death. "Don't be stupid, he's dead," he said. "I know he's dead," Samantha replied, "but he came to my bedroom and said he was going to heaven and he had come to say goodbye." She told her brother she had seen that his hands and face were burned and said she would kiss them better. But he had told her, "Don't worry, I'll be better soon."

'About six weeks later I went to a spiritualist church some ten miles away from my home. The medium, Kitty, said there was someone present who had helped a boy who had been burned to death. I was still pretty upset about it all and didn't really want to know but my friend nudged me. The medium described how I had seen Paul and even what my daughter had said. At that point, I hadn't told anyone what had happened and was beginning to wonder if it was all my imagination, but this was proof to me. I have seen Paul since at a different spiritualist church. I had been on shift work and was pretty tired. The medium was quite good but I was wishing I hadn't gone. Then I saw Paul standing by me. I said to myself, "I'll only believe this if the medium says something." Then Paul began talking to me and the medium said,

"You've got a blonde boy standing next to you." I replied, "It's OK, I've got the message."

'One of the things he asked me was to tell his mum he was okay now. The strange thing was that he was standing there with no clothes on with a friend of mine who'd died about ten years before and they were laughing at my puzzlement. Then, when I was thinking it over, I worked it out. Paul's body had been almost completely destroyed by the fire, even the soles of his feet. When I saw him, there wasn't a mark on his body. That's what he wanted me to tell his mum.

'I tried to talk to his mum but I realised she didn't want to hear so I shut up about it. I felt Paul around our house for about a year afterwards and heard him in the hallway. He isn't around now but the Christmas after he died, he was there sure enough helping my seven-year old on his new flipper football game – with two of them against one of us they were winning every time.'

The ties that bind parents to their dead children may have started long before those children were born. Norah told me: 'I believe that there is evidence of a psychic bond between my son and I that predates his birth and extends beyond his death. As soon as I was pregnant, I knew that I was carrying a boy. I had no medical evidence for this. It was just something I felt. On and off throughout pregnancy, it seemed to me that I was visited by my son-to-be. I can only describe this by explaining that it felt as though I was not alone (when apparently I was) or if I was in company that an extra presence was with us. At other times I would feel that the spirit of my baby was not around and would say to my husband, "I feel as though the baby has gone off again." Over the nine months of my pregnancy, I began to pick up on certain qualities or characteristics to get a sense of what my son would be like and found these to be quite accurate after he was born and had begun to display more of his personality to us.

'I am not a psychic person, nor a particularly sensitive one. But so certain was I that I was carrying a boy, that I did not bother to think about girls' names at all. For a while during the pregnancy, I thought we might call him Caleb. Then, one night when I was about seven months pregnant, I dreamt I'd given birth and the baby was a boy. He was wrapped in a white blanket and I was looking down at him. He looked up at me with clear direct eyes and said, "Well, what are you going to call me then?" I told him rather hesitantly that we were thinking of calling him Caleb and he replied very assertively, "Oh, I'm not having that and I don't want any Indian name either."

'On the day he was born, we went for a walk to get some contractions moving. While we were walking, I found myself overcome with a mixture of fear and sadness. It centred around the fear that at the end of this particular pregnancy there was not going to be a baby for me. I had a definite sense of foreboding that in some way he would be taken away from me. At the time, it seemed totally irrational although very real and I put it down to hormonal changes. Though after his death, it seemed to me that I had always known that I wouldn't be able to keep him. Joel died in November totally unexpectedly from a cot death. Finding him dead shocked me to the core and yet looking back on his last week alive, it seems to me now that both he and I knew his life was about to end. When he died he was about six-and-a-half months old. Though he was taking some solids, he was still breastfeeding. I loved feeding him and he never showed any signs that he was losing interest. Then one morning about five days before his death, he refused. He wasn't unhappy or ill. He would still take formula milk or even my milk so long as it was from a bottle. I was absolutely distraught. It felt as though he was rejecting me, leaving me, telling me our special time together was over. I said to Doug, "I feel as though I'm grieving" and that's how it was over the next few days.

'After Joel did die, I felt grateful to him for weaning himself like that. It seems clear to me that he was beginning to separate himself from me, preparing us both and especially me for his death. Having had to do some letting go of him that week definitely softened the wrench that I felt when he died, because by that time I had come to accept that I could not hold onto Joel. On the morning of his funeral, I drained the last of my milk and poured it down the sink.

'On the day before he died, I can see, looking back that there were definite messages for me that it was going to be his last day. In the mornings, I usually got on with the household chores while Joel played in the same room. This normally seemed fine for both of us, but that day, it kept coming to me again and again, like a voice in my head, that I should forget about the chores for that day and just enjoy being with Joel. There was a softness around us both that day. I felt quite mesmerised by him and dreamy and spent more time than usual with him.

'Evening came and he'd got quite grubby but I was behind with supper and getting ready to go out, so I decided to leave him as he was and clean him up in the morning. While I was cooking I suddenly remembered a saying of my mum's that you should always go out in clean underwear in case you had an accident. Suddenly I felt like I had to clean Joel up. I lay him by the fire in the kitchen and bathed him from head to toe which he loved. As I dressed him in clean clothes I explained to him I wouldn't have wanted anyone to see him looking so dirty. There was no reason for me to suspect at the time that anyone would see him like that and yet again it was almost as if I knew. It may seem like a small detail, but it was a source of great relief to me that when we took him to the children's hospital, the next day, he was looking clean and cared for and that I had given him that final wash and he had not died dirty.

'After we'd had our supper, I gave Joel his last bottle. Often he would reach up with one hand and pull at my hair in quite a rough way, but on this night he was quite different. As he sucked earnestly on his bottle, he reached up with one hand and stroked the length of my face, running his fingers over my eyes, nose, mouth and hair in a very adult and loving way, very slowly and carefully, gently repeating the movement many times. I had a crick in my neck, because my head was bent forward for him to reach it, but I could not bring myself to move in case I interrupted this moment. Again there was a voice in my head reminding me to enjoy him for now. It was his touch and the way he looked at me that left me feeling that my absolute love for him was totally reciprocated. Recalling those moments now it also seems to me that he was reminding himself of my face, touching me one last time as though he also knew he was saying goodbye to me. Later Doug was settling Joel down for the night when I had an overwhelming desire to have a cuddle with him. Part of

me said to myself this was ridiculous, that I would un-
settle him just as he was going off to sleep, but it was so
strong that I stopped Doug from putting him down and
picked Joel up for one last hug.

'Ever since Joel's birth he had been our alarm. But the
next morning we woke up later than usual and there was
silence. I said to Doug, "What about Joel?" and even
before Doug went into his room, I knew he was dead. For
his coffin, we had a cross made of white roses and carna-
tions and after the funeral we brought it home and put it
by the front door to our house. One day I came in and
touched one of the roses as I passed the front door. As I
did I thought of Joel. Suddenly something burst into life
– it seemed to come into being from within me and
around me at the same time and just kept expanding to
fill the whole hallway. I felt full of joy and ran up the stairs
to the room where Joel had died. I couldn't see anything,
yet I sensed this presence as being warm and golden. I
"knew" that it was Joel.

'My husband also received a visit from Joel in the week
that followed his death and also experienced a very large
presence. There was a very strange quality to the days
that followed Joel's death. On one level it was a night-
mare too awful to be true. Yet the engulfing darkness of
those early days was pierced somehow by a light, a feeling
of grace in the house and around us. There were times we
felt as if we were floating, even flying. We lost our baby,
but we gained in knowledge. Finding Joel's dead body,
collecting his ashes and seeing this plastic bag of char-
coal that was all that was left of our beautiful son . . . and
yet on another level, I knew beyond a tremor of a doubt
that Joel's life was not an ending, but somehow a begin-

ning. It was as though in dying, in making a transition from the physical to the spiritual, Joel opened up a door for me between these two realities. Though I remained in the physical, for a while the spiritual remained more real to me. Joel passed from the visible into the invisible and there are times when I feel that actually these two worlds exist in the same space and if I knew how to cross the boundary between them, I could reach out and touch him.'

Robbie was only 13 when an exploratory operation discovered the extent of the brain tumour which eventually would kill him. Margaret, his mother, told me: 'The loss of a child, who one minute is dancing up and down in front of you and organising games for all the other kids, and then the next minute is struck down by an obscene growth in his head – how can you accept such a loss unless there is something more beyond this life? So much life and fun as Robbie had must go on beyond the grave. With old people, you can say at least they lived their lives, but with a child it's not fair. He hasn't had a chance.'

His surgeon had said there was nothing they could do and that Robbie had six months to live. Margaret took him home but was told he had to go back to hospital again for radium treatment. Although she was a trained nurse, Margaret decided to take him to a psychic healer. As she said: 'At that stage, you try anything. On the way home after his first visit, Robbie was very quiet. "You're not going to believe this, mum," he said. "I was lying there and you know the pictures of Jesus with the cloak – well, he was standing there. I looked at his face, he opened his cloak and both my grandads were standing there too. I was absolutely terrified and closed my eyes.

When I opened them they were still there. It's stupid –
why should I see my grandads when they're both dead?
And when Eileen [the healer] put me on my tummy,
gradually I realised someone had come and put a hand on
my back between my shoulders. It was warm. I knew it
wasn't Eileen. I thought as I had seen Jesus, it might have
been him, but that's silly, isn't it?"'

Margaret's husband nearly went up the wall when she
told him what Robbie had said. 'It must be the drugs,' he
insisted. The drugs that Robbie had had to start taking
gradually destroyed the nerves in his ears and legs. Then
Margaret herself started trying to practise psychic healing. Said Margaret: 'I used to put my hands round his
head. He said it felt lovely and warm. But I could feel the
obscene tumour in his head and I had the feeling I
couldn't heal him, though it always made him more
settled.' But Robbie's tumour was spreading down the
brain stem. Margaret consulted another healer, but
eventually lost faith in him after she was told, while waiting for the results of Robbie's latest brain scan, 'You will
be thrilled with the results of the scan. Robbie will be
fine.' When they went back to the hospital, the doctors
said they were sorry but Robbie only had four months
left. However, Robbie had lasted far longer than the
original medical prognosis said he would and remained
active when he should have become paralysed, so Margaret feels the healing from various sources was not totally
in vain. What she condemns is the raising of false hope.
'It is wrong to offer hope of a miracle.'

On New Year's Eve, the family were playing cards at
home when Robbie cried, 'Mum there's something terrible in my head.' By this time, his body had no temper-

ature control and after three days of dreadful fits, he was admitted to hospital again. They were told he could not last the night, but although he continued to have fits off and on for almost 56 hours, he survived. At this stage he no longer recognised his mother, calling her the 'nice lady who comes to see me', though he still recognised his dad. Unable to bear any more, Margaret went to the hospital chapel. Opening a bible at random, she saw the quotation: 'The Lord shall give thee one more day'. Then she went back to the ward to hear Robbie saying, 'There's my mum. I'd know her footsteps anywhere. Hello mum.' It was then she realised that he had gone blind. Fortunately his sight came back and Margaret considers it a small miracle that he knew her till the end.

He then began to have trouble with his left hand, his chemical balance went and he was ragged with dehydration. Margaret asked the nurse to sedate him as nothing more could be done. The nurse insisted she had a rest, so Margaret wandered over to the parents' flat and started to iron her husband's shirt for the next day. A tune kept running through her head, over and over again. At first she couldn't place it then she realised it was 'The day thou gavest lord is ended'. She left the shirt and rushed to Robbie. It was the start of the rundown to his death. Margaret sat all night by his bed. There was no response, but whenever she took her hand away, he grabbed it hard. Gradually Robbie slipped away.

Three days after his death, Margaret believes she saw Robbie in his bedroom. He was wearing what the family used to jokingly call his Rupert Bear trousers. He was getting something off the top of his tallboy where he kept all his treasures. He had grown. The radium treatment had stopped his spine growing so his legs had grown but not his body. Now he appeared to have grown normally. He smiled at Margaret who was so shocked she burst into tears and ran away.

Lindsey, Robbie's four-year-old sister also saw her brother after his death. She is now nearly fourteen, but can still remember Robbie coming back to see her. 'Before he died, Robbie was always organising games for us. He was great fun. Sometimes we used to play schools and he would be the teacher. He was always making us laugh. Once at the old house, after Robbie died, I was wandering around with nothing to do. I was by myself and lonely and Robbie turned up. I spoke to him and played with him. He made me laugh. He came several times after that, when I was alone.

'Then when I was six or seven and we had moved to our new house, I went into my friend Nick's sitting room. Nick said, "I'll get my new train set" and disappeared upstairs. I heard someone coming downstairs a few minutes afterwards. I thought it was Nicky and I said, "Hurry up." But when I looked round, it was Robbie sitting next to me. I told Nick, but he made fun of me and told my mum, "Guess what Lindsey said she saw at my house."'

Robbie had always been the first into his parents' bedroom in the morning every Christmas, birthday, Mother's Day or Father's Day to ask eagerly, 'Is it time yet?' and wake them up by bouncing on the bed. After he died, Margaret told me, this did not stop. The first time it happened, her husband thought it was Margaret who had got up early to make a cup of tea, but she was still in bed. On every special occasion, Margaret says she still feels the pressure of the bed going down. Things on the television would be rearranged as well and as Robbie had always liked to tease his mother, Margaret is convinced that this is him, playing games with them. Her husband hates her to wear curlers in bed, telling her, 'If I woke up and saw you like that I'd die with fright.' It's a family joke. One night after Robbie had died, Margaret had a special interview the next day and was anxious to look her best, so she pinned up the front of her hair and was just putting on a net to hold it in place. As she surveyed herself in the bathroom mirror, she heard Robbie's voice in her ear: 'Now who's going to frighten who then?' She tells me that it was exactly Robbie's humour. As Margaret said: 'All that life and fun couldn't be here one minute and then just gone.'

I had been talking to Margaret in the kitchen of her house. Her daughter Lindsey had been playing with my three-year-old Miranda, who was not far off the age Lindsey was when Robbie died. On the way home, Miranda said to me, 'I liked the swing in the garden.' When I telephoned Margaret some time later, I mentioned this. 'We haven't got one in this garden,' she said, 'but we used to have one at the old house though.'

7

Invisible Friends

Most children have invisible companions at some stage of their lives. We currently share our house with Mr Teddy, a huge invisible bear that lives under eight-year-old Jade's bed and comes from Spain, Jack's friend Mr God who, we are assured by Jack, goes round in his hot air balloon at night switching off the sky so people can go to sleep and odd members of three-year-old Miranda's squirrel family – she informed us one day that she was really a squirrel whose tree had blown down so she had to come and live with us!

This is not an exceptional state of affairs nor anything to get worried about. Surveys[*] have shown that about a fifth of young children seem to have permanent invisible companions and that this phenomenon depends more on

---

[*] Separate studies were carried out by the psychologists Elizabeth and John Newson (see their book *Four Years Old in an Urban Community*, Penguin, 1976) and the Yale Guidance Nursery (see *The Normal Child* by C W Valentine, Penguin, 1967).

the child's temperament than on loneliness. Among gifted children the proportion rises steeply. The psychologist Lewis Terman found that of 554 gifted children aged between five and thirteen, 72 per cent of girls and 37 per cent of boys had permanent invisible companions. Perhaps intelligent, creative children find they have less in common with their contemporaries and find companions they create more satisfying. And, as the psychologists Elizabeth and John Newson point out, invisible friends always score over real ones in that they are always available, always friendly and will go away when you want them to without ever getting offended.

There might be some cause for alarm in the family, however, if a child's belief in invisible friends persisted into adult life. After all, adults are supposed to live in a rational world where they believe in only what they can touch and see, a world that can be measured and which runs by carefully laid down scientific principles. Therefore we also need reassurance that the invisible friends are only figments of a childish imagination, though there is evidence worth considering that some invisible friends might be more than just that.

Jan is now a mother of three children but she still remembers and believes in the existence of her childhood invisible friend, a girl named Jellot. Her first recollection of Jellot goes back to when she was sitting in a huge black pram. 'Jellot was pushing the pram with my mother. I used to point at the empty space at the end of the pram.'

Jan's mother was always very worried by Jellot and constantly emphasised that Jan's friend was imaginary. In their survey (see footnote, page 97), Elizabeth and John Newson found that many mothers were disturbed by their children's invisible friends and a few feared it might be a sign of mental instability. But where a mother was prepared to accept a child's fantasies at face value and enter into his or her imaginative world, she might stimulate further fantasies or develop those the child already had. This is not necessarily a bad thing. For children to grow up confident and with a sense of worth, they need to have all their experiences treated with the importance they themselves attach to them.

Jan next remembers Jellot when she was two or slightly older. 'There were two air-raid shelters at the bottom of the garden and two men came to see if they were safe. This would be in 1950 or 1951. They decided they were and cleaned them out. The shelters were brick built and you went down steps to them. I used them as a Wendy house and dad bricked up the entrance to the alley so I could play safely. Jellot lived in the shelters. I used to have to walk her back there when she had come shopping with me. I can still visualise her clearly. She wore clothes that weren't like mine. They were old-fashioned and her brown dress used to come down below her knee. You could see it under her coat which she always kept buttoned up even at the table. She wore a double-breasted camel coat with a collar. It was a rich material and soft to touch. She had brown shoes with buttons.'

Jan used to try to make her mum hold her hand out for Jellot when they went out and used to scream because she wouldn't. Her aunty always did this though and her dad would sometimes lay a place at the table for Jellot. Jan says that Jellot's hand felt warm to her and could be held like anyone else's. Jellot always had one sock rolled down and had curly blonde flyaway hair. 'She was always with me. Everybody in the road knew Jellot and when I played with the other kids in the street, Jellot would come too. When it was Jellot's turn to skip, the kids used to turn the empty rope. They tolerated her and I was under the impression they must also be able to see her because I could.'

The willingness of the other children in the street to accept Jellot's existence is not in itself proof of her reality. Children are usually quite happy to share the fantasy worlds of others. But some evidence came in a later incident. 'One day I was sitting with mum in our small front room, listening to *Listen with Mother* on the radio. I was about four. I remember mum was knitting a pink cardigan. There was a knock at the door and I went to answer it. Mum told me off for wandering away. "I thought you were listening to your programme," she protested. She hadn't heard the knock. I turned the big door handle, opened the door and Jellot was standing there with a woman. "Oh hello, Jellot," I said. Then the woman with Jellot told me that Aunty Bea [she was the old lady who lived across the road] had died and I turned to my mum and said, "Mum, why has Aunty Bea died?" Mum told me not to be silly, but after *Listen with Mother*, she went over the road to see Aunty Bea's next door neighbour and asked her if she'd seen the old lady. She hadn't which was unusual and the neighbour went off to phone Aunty Bea's brother to see if she had gone there for the day. Mum wasn't involved in that but the neighbour came over later in the afternoon to say that Aunty had died in the night and they had found the body.'

How could Jan have known that Aunty Bea was dead if no one else knew, unless she was told by her invisible friends? One possible explanation is put forward by Dr Keith Harary, an American psychologist and parapsychologist who has had numerous psychic experiences himself (he was tested extensively as a teenager for an ability to leave his body and send his spirit travelling). During his childhood he had various invisible friends who seemed to give him help in developing his psychic powers. But later he wrote: 'My childhood (imaginary) friends sometimes seemed real to me in the sense they would provide me with information to which I would not have normally had access. However, I do not believe they existed separately from my own internal processes.'[*] Rather, he believed they served as a means of expression for his own emerging psychic powers.

But this only raises the question that if Jellot was not real, is Jan psychic? She told me about two experiences of telepathy involving her sons. She was working as a swimming teacher and on Thursdays would stay late at the baths. A friend took her children home and gave them tea. But one particular Thursday, Jan had an urgent feeling that she should go home early. It was so acute, she says, that she would have walked out if her supervisor had not agreed to let her go. At about 1.25pm when Jan was telling her supervisor that she could not stay late, her son Ian, then aged eight, fell badly on the ice at school and sustained a hairline fracture. The school, not realising how badly he was hurt, did not send him home and even allowed him to go to sleep, a dangerous thing to do in a case of concussion. At the end of the day Jan's friend came to take Ian home and was astonished to see Jan's

[*] This comes from a letter to the *Journal of the Society for Psychical Research*, January 1989.

car draw up at the same time she arrived. 'What are you doing here?' she asked in amazement and relief as Ian was looking very poorly. 'I think I know what I'm doing here,' replied Jan. Ian was taken to hospital and stayed there for two days. As with cases of telepathy I have mentioned in Chapter 2, Jan had changed her course without logical reason and had been there to offer her support to her distressed and badly injured child.

Jan's other experience was with her elder son Robert when he was 14. She can date it precisely to Tuesday June 13, 1989, as he was then due to have a TB innoculation at school. Jan had an appointment with someone at 11 am but Robert had no idea at what time he would be given the injection. Jan's visitor arrived 10 minutes late and as he walked through the door, Jan grabbed her arm and said 'ouch' for no apparent reason. That night she asked Robert if the injection hurt. 'Did it hurt, mum!' he replied. 'I'll say it did!' Robert then went on to tell her he had had the injection at exactly 11.10am. He had been looking at his watch at the time to see how many seconds it took.

Jellot began to fade out of Jan's life when she started school. 'I didn't have time then to go down to the air-raid shelters any more. Then when I was seven they took down part of the shelters and took the roof off and only left them as a wall. Jellot stopped coming after that.'

But if Jellot faded away, 30 years later another invisible friend entered Jan's life, and again the friend appeared to be able to provide the child involved with unexpected information. Jan's son Ian had a companion who apparently came from the France of several hundred years ago. Because her mother had been so discouraging about

Jellot, Jan was determined that it should be different for Ian and she came to regard the invisible Andrix (the spelling of his name is phonetic) as almost another child, the member of the family who was always there though he could only be seen by Ian.

From the beginning Jan believed that Ian could really seen Andrix because she had really seen Jellot. She recalls that Andrix first appeared when Ian was barely two years old. He was walking and starting to talk and play in an organised fashion. He used to sit on the floor playing at handing toys to someone who was not there and calling out his invisible friend's name. Jan points out that Ian was not a solitary child, since he had his brother Robert who was fourteen months older and later, a younger sister. But of the three, only Ian had an invisible playmate.

When Ian was a little older, Jan was sitting on the floor playing with him when he suddenly said, 'Oops squashed.' Ian couldn't explain at the time what he meant, but later told his mother that she had sat on Andrix. Then when Ian was nearly four, he tried to tell Jan what Andrix was wearing. They had a velvet pile settee and Ian used to run his fingers down the pile and say, 'That feels like Andrix's coat – that looks like Andrix's coat.' Jan says he was referring to the different colours you get when you smooth the pile. Andrix wore short trousers to the knee, very thin socks and shiny shoes. Ian told his mother Andrix was French. 'How can you understand French then?' asked Jan. 'When you go to the other place everyone talks the same,' Ian replied. Jan was astonished to hear this coming from a four-year-old. She then said a few French words to Ian to see if he understood them but he didn't. The family's first visit to France did not take place until a year later when Ian was five.

One evening, Jan found Ian in his bedroom, apparently talking to Andrix. He was saying, 'It's all right, she's downstairs. She can't hear you. No, she won't come up, honestly.' When talking to Andrix, Ian would leave gaps as if Andrix was replying. The next morning, Jan found all Ian's toy cars with their bonnets up. Ian explained, 'Andrix doesn't know what an engine is so I have to show him. They didn't have engines in those days. There wasn't an engine on horses, but you have horse power don't you?'

Jan's husband used to make model planes and Ian had several, including a model of Concorde, on display in his bedroom. 'The next evening,' says Jan, 'I heard a noise, but didn't investigate. In the morning I noticed the nose was broken off Concorde. I was cross with Ian as he was not destructive and he was really upset. "Andrix did it," he insisted. "He was trying to find the engine and tried to lift the bonnet and it broke." "But planes don't have engines under the bonnet," I explained. "I know that," said Ian, "but Andrix doesn't."'

When Ian was almost five he suddenly came out with the words – uncommon for a child of his age – 'cart ruts'. Apparently, Andrix had told Ian that he had once fallen into a cart track. He was crossing over the road when he tripped on the ruts. 'It was very deep, mummy,' Ian said. 'The mud actually came up to Andrix's waist.' He also informed Jan that the roads were always muddy in Andrix's time and that they used to put sacking under the cart wheels to stop them sticking in the ruts.

A few months later, Ian's older brother, Robert, was given a fountain pen to improve his writing. This pen apparently fascinated Andrix who told Ian he used to write with feathers, though Ian had no idea at the time what a quill pen was. One morning Jan found a squashed ink cartridge and ink all over Ian's bed and room. But, she said, there was not a drop of ink on Ian. 'Andrix was trying to find out how it worked,' Ian explained.

I asked Jan if Ian ever saw the *Three Musketeers* or similar programmes on television when he was young. She said that he hadn't and that they didn't have television on very much when he was that age. Ian had mostly grown up on a diet of *Thomas the Tank Engine*, and they had certainly not been to France when Andrix first appeared. She cannot remember them even talking about France.

Once Ian started school, he began to go to bed earlier. He then told Jan that Andrix got very angry and used to say, 'You don't want to be my friend any more.' Ian wanted Andrix to go to school with him, but apparently Andrix said he couldn't as he wasn't allowed to leave Ian's room. Andrix then seemed to disappear for about three months. Then he reappeared and disappeared again for a while, then came back and finally came no more. Jan dates his final disappearance to the time they moved to their present house when Ian was just turned seven.

Ian was almost thirteen when he talked to me about Andrix in July 1989. 'Andrix spoke French and another language so that everyone could understand him. He was always my best friend. I could see him and feel him. Whatever happened in the day, if I was told off or if I was angry with dad or in a bad mood or if I was sad, I could tell Andrix and he would put it all right by the morning. He had brown hair with a strange parting flicked over to the left side. Andrix solved all my problems. I would run to my bedroom and draw a picture of whoever I had fallen out with. Then Andrix told me to cross the person out and in the morning everything would be all right. Andrix would tell me I should be loving, kind and forgiving. Andrix came from far away where it was muddy, he was always muddy. Once I lost my set of cars. In a dream I had, Andrix had found them and they were there the next morning.

'Andrix was like me inside except that he was magic. He was a magic me. Sometimes I miss Andrix and wish I had him again. I have got even more problems now. He was a true friend. I think of him as a friend and a brother. He was a nuisance sometimes, but he was always very interesting.'

Jan says she used to take up drinks and biscuits for Andrix. 'I treated Andrix as if he were real and talked about him to Ian because as a girl I had been inhibited from talking about Jellot. When Andrix finally went, I was sad.' Jan feels losing Andrix was for her almost like losing a child, for Andrix was a part of her life as well as Ian's. Though Jan never spoke to him and is positive she never saw him, she says she could always visualise Andrix and felt she knew him. To her, invisible friends are entirely positive and she thinks Andrix gave the family serenity and tranquillity and had a calming presence. Jan says she felt a sense of continuity and that 'someone was sharing our lives in the same way as Jellot had shared my life as a child.' She tried to explain: 'Andrix was the part of me that played with Ian. He was able to give Ian the time that I couldn't, because I was busy with two small children and a husband working nights.'

Jan firmly believes that Andrix and Jellot are connected and were real, not imaginary. Jan and Ian still talk about Jellot and Andrix as if they are living but absent family members. She believes that Jellot moved on to another child who needed her more and Ian thinks Andrix is with someone else too. 'We grow up, but they stay the same,' said Jan. 'We only see these people at a certain age. The invisible friends were there in childhood when we needed them and then someone else needs them more.'

This belief was echoed by Carolyn, who told me that as a child, she had an imaginary friend called Jockson who came from Australia and had to share everything with her. Her mother went along with it and Jockson lasted until she started school, but Carolyn, now in her thirties says she can still recall him clearly. She also told me that a few years ago, she met a woman who had had a child late in life. This little girl was very advanced and the mother found her hard to cope with. She also found it hard to cope with the little girl's invisible friend, a dark-haired little boy called Jackson whose description matched that of Carolyn's Jockson. Carolyn cannot help thinking it is her friend, come back to another child twenty years later.

Neither Jan or Carolyn are spiritualists. But their feelings about their invisible friends parallel the spiritualist belief that invisible friends can be companions from the spirit world. Ann Bennett of Gloucester Spiritualist Church told me about the spirit of a tall coloured gentleman who was close to her son and daughter from a very early age. 'My daughter saw him on several occasions.

When she was small, we had very high bunk beds and one night she was very feverish. But I was amazed the next morning to find her completely better. She told me that in the night a black man had come to see her and he must have been very tall to reach her on the top bunk. She kept on about him throughout her childhood and was later told by a medium that a tall coloured gentleman called Theobald was looking after her.'

Lots of quite ordinary children have invisible friends who are 'super-versions' of themselves who can do everything the child is afraid of or unable to do. In other cases the invisible friend could be the one who gets the blame – very conveniently as he cannot answer back – for all the mischief that goes on. Under certain conditions, a mother can actively help her child to construct an imaginary companion and the family therapist, Helen Manning considers that such joint constructions might have the pay-off of providing company for the child and result in a closer relationship between the child and the mother.

Whether or not they can help to heal the body or offer good advice in times of trouble, the value of invisible companions would seem to be great in helping a child to cope with both social and emotional difficulties. Even Piaget, who believed imagination stemmed only from what a child had lived through and that the child grew out of fantasy as he became intellectually adapted to the real world, admitted the value of imaginary companions. His daughter Jacqueline had, among other friends, a strange bird-like creature that helped her in all she learned, gave her encouragement and consoled her when she was sad. In fact, invisible friends do not have to be in human form and, like Jacqueline, between the ages of three and six, Chrissie had an animal friend – an invisible chicken that nested at the end of her bed. 'How do you know what the chicken is saying when he just clucks?' her mother had asked. Chrissie's reply had been very smug – 'When you learn it, mummy, you will speak in the same language as it does.'

Invisible friends can be quite exotic, triggered perhaps by a particularly vivid picture. Greta, who is now 79, can still recall her special friends, two small Indian gentlemen, that she knew when she was five. 'I may have seen a picture in a children's magazine,' she wrote, 'but these were not at all wild-looking. They were very tidy indeed and very quiet. They were dressed in white dhotis and shawls and I would give tea parties for them at which they sat rather uncomfortably on chairs cross-legged.' During her childhood, Greta had no connection with India, but later she became very involved in the cause of Indian independence, had a vision of Ghandi in prison and finally in 1965 spent two months in India. She says, 'I was greeted by Hindu friends as one of them. I reject a belief in reincarnation, but they were sure I had come home.'

Worried parents might take invisible friends to be a sign of a child's instability. The psychologist Michael Jackson, who has been researching the link between spiritual experiences and psychoses, does not believe that such problems are that simple, but he says that people who are likely to have valid psychic experiences are usually of a sensitive temperament and, as many psychoses are believed to stem from over-sensitivity, they may be wrongly labelled as psychotic. Another expert believes that children who have had valid psychic experiences may be wrongly diagnosed as epileptics and spend years on unnecessary drugs. One such child was Rachel who from a pre-school age would walk round in circles and appear to 'speak in tongues' in a strange language that had the rhythm and punctuation of normal speech. Afterwards she would remember nothing. At five she was diagnosed as having *petit mal* and was given drugs that seemed to reduce her to a pale shadow of her former self. This happened 20 years ago and attitudes now hopefully are more enlightened.

Sometimes people with psychotic problems in later life, had invisible friends as children, though that doesn't necessarily imply a link between the two. Nick, now thirty-five, spent half of his twenties in hospital diagnosed as a paranoid schizophrenic. Whether his condition was caused by his childhood problems or whether he had a predisposition to mental illness is a matter for psychiatrists, but his story is quite moving. At a very early age, he was taken to Canada by his mother to find his father, a Canadian working in Winnipeg. They eventually met up and when Nick was two, his parents married. For a time the family were happy.

After Nick's first day at school when he was six, he saw a boy standing at the bottom of his bed wearing a school cap and a badge. Nick remembers the badge had a thick J with a thin S coiling round it like a snake. 'Who are you?' he asked. 'I'm your friend,' replied the boy. They spent hours playing together but the friend said Nick must not tell his parents because it was a secret. He kept saying 'In England we do this – in England we wear that.' Nick asked what he was doing in Canada if he went to school in England and the boy replied, 'You brought me from England. When you go back, we'll go back together.'

Nick's mother died in an accident when he was about seven and after the funeral, Nick found his invisible friend standing in his bedroom with a suitcase. Nick's dad was working as a ranch hand and could not keep him, so after six months he was sent to stay with his grandparents in England. Nick travelled alone except for his invisible friend. When the boat arrived in England, the boy got off the boat as well and Nick never saw him again.

Cathy, diagnosed as a manic depressive, was in a mental hospital for 28 years. She says that from the age of two-and-half she had two invisible girlfriends. One had very dark hair, which had been cut short because she had nits. The other girl had long blonde hair with a blue bow, which the dark-haired girl was always trying to untie. Her mum used to shout at her for jigging about in the middle of the room, but Cathy says she was only trying to stop them fighting over the bow. Cathy's invisible friends disappeared when she went to school, which was a relief as she had been worried about how to stop them fighting in class. Also, Cathy's friends would say to her: 'Did you know there's dust under that vase?' or 'Did you know the cat has torn the curtains?' She would tell her mother who would then blame Cathy saying, 'You must have done it if you knew about it.'

The most exciting and perhaps the elusive invisible friends are the fairy folk. Julie recalls that, as a child, she had a big garden and in the part of it where she played were little spirit friends who were like fairies. To Julie, they were not just pretend friends. Indeed, she says she has seen them in adult life, especially in a particular place in Devon. 'My own children have seen them too. Once when we were together, we all saw them. My eldest son was nine and the youngest only about four at the time.' 'What are they like?' I asked her. 'They are very fleeting,' she replied, 'like butterflies, but not as small. In fact, they are about the size of squirrels.'

The most famous case of 'fairies at the bottom of the garden' is probably the Cottingley affair over which there is still controversy more than 70 years later. In 1917, cousins Frances Griffiths, then aged eleven, and Elsie Wright, then aged sixteen, claimed to have played with fairies in a glen at Cottingley in the Yorkshire dales. They produced photographs which baffled the experts including Kodak and Sir Arthur Conan Doyle, the creator of Sherlock Holmes. One photograph showed a group of fairy-like figures dancing in front of a girl, the other a winged gnome-like creature near a girl's beckoning hand. Some 60 years later, the cousins admitted that four of the photographs had been faked, but this is not the end of the story because Frances said that they did take one genuine photograph. She told Joe Cooper, a psychic researcher: 'It was a wet Saturday afternoon and we were just mooching about with our cameras and Elsie had nothing prepared. I saw these fairies building up in the grasses and just aimed the camera and took a photograph.'

Elsie, however, insisted that *all* the photographs were fakes. But like Frances, she claimed that there actually were fairies. She said that the reason they had faked the pictures were to prove to jeering adults that the fairy folk did exist. Perhaps many of the so-called 'child frauds' result from the demands of doubting adults for a child to prove any out-of-the-ordinary experience.

Children have been entranced by fairies for generations though they are more of a rural or at least big garden phenomena. Pat, for example, used to see fairies when she was about four, at the bottom of the garden belonging to the old lady who helped to bring her up. 'It was a big garden with a stream running at the bottom. The fairies were very tiny, dressed in pink gossamer and used to play around by the stream. I told them my wildest dreams. They used to fly and hover with their tiny wings. I did not tell anyone as I knew they would have laughed.' And Felicity, a psychology student, remembers a field near her house in the country where as a child 'I used to see fairies in the long-grass. They were a greeny-blue colour, but they were typical fairies. They used to talk to me. At the time I never told anyone. I was convinced they were real at the time, though looking back now I think they may have been projections of my imagination. When we moved, when my parents were divorced, there wasn't a field so I did not see them any more.'

Fairies seem to have faded with the sprawl of the suburbs. The children of today that I talked to had hardly come across them at all. Perhaps there is not enough room in the gardens of the new estate houses for fairies to spread their wings properly. However, if a new and more compact breed of fairy, tougher and more suited to inner city life has emerged anywhere and been spotted by children, I would certainly love to hear about them.

Fairy Godmothers and Guardian Angels

Good fairies, angels and fairy godmothers are regarded by some psychologists as a children's way of coping with the fearsome elements in their lives, many of which are not real dangers but come from their own fantasies and their sense of helplessness against powerful adults. They can also be seen as a way of splitting the good and bad elements which a young child finds hard to accept as co-existing in the same person. The bad fairy, created out of these bad feelings, can stand in for the side of mummy that blows her top at her child, when at the end of a long hard day he empties the contents of the cornflakes packet all over the kitchen floor. It helps to ease the way at a time when children cannot understand that even a loving mother can be bad-tempered and unloving at times.

Slowly children learn that love and hate can co-exist – in moderation – and that it is safe at times to hate mother without either destroying her or themselves. But in the meantime they learn to project their fears and anger into

the person of the wicked witch who can be overcome by
the good fairy. Melanie Klein[*] tells of a six-year-old boy
who made her play the alternating roles of fairy mamma
and bad mamma. 'Whenever the fairy mamma goes out
of the room,' he said, 'you never know whether she won't
come back all of a sudden as the bad mamma.' This boy
had psychological problems but elements of his idea of a
good and bad mamma are present in all children. So it is
not surprising that children need to call up helpful ghosts
or voices to load the dice of life more in their favour and
that those who feel their call has been answered are
firmly convinced it is *not* all in the mind.

Pauline believed that a voice intervened twice on her
behalf when she was a child. The first time was in 1930
when she was ten and the fourth child of a family of eight.
'Dad was out of work and my mother was always struggling to make ends meet. The constant worry made her
sharp-tongued and quick with a cuff round the ear if we
didn't jump to do what she said. Each evening after
school, it was always my job to look after my baby
brother. Mother gave me instructions to take him in his
pram and push him round the streets so he got some fresh
air, but once I disobeyed her. On that occasion, as soon as
she disappeared into the house, I pushed the baby down
the yard, turned a corner where we would not be seen and
left him safely outside while I entered the old wash house.
I was determined to do something an older brother had
told me about the day before. I had to stand on a wobbly
bucket to reach the communal cold tap that served our
family and three others. I turned it on and put my finger

* See *The Psycho-Analysis of Children* by Melanie Klein, Virago, 1989.

inside making the water squirt out all over the place. I was so engrossed in this wonderful game that I was lost to the world. But suddenly a loud clear voice in my ear said, "Your mother is coming down the yard into the wash house. Get out quick."

'I was so startled that I fell off the bucket. I picked myself up and ran to where I had left the baby and we quickly hid behind the privy wall. Luckily the baby was quiet. Then my mother came and filled the old iron kettle in the wash house. That voice saved me from a good hiding.'

Pauline, like many children from poorer families at that time had to adopt an adult role that clashed with her childish desires. Her adult side was obviously very strong (backed up with the threat of a clout from her mother if she misbehaved) but for once her childish instinct decided to have a good time. Perhaps common sense was struggling to reconcile the two. Pauline knew that her mother often came into the wash house to fill the kettle or do some sort of task and that it was quite likely she would get caught. Maybe she instinctively felt deep down that an authoritative warning was needed to restore order. Were the words: 'Your mother is coming' produced by the adult part of Pauline's mind? Or was there some benign essence passing by, who was glad that Pauline was able to be a child for once and didn't want her to get a thrashing?

Pauline's second voice came to help out when she was about twelve. 'Dad was still out of work and things were desperate at home. He had a pair of worn-out boots, his only ones. He used to mend all the family's shoes expertly on an iron foot, but at the time just could not afford to buy a sixpenny piece of leather from the cobbler's. I was on an urgent errand to the Co-op for three pennyworth of bacon and was thinking about Dad as I hurried along. I was walking on some broken pavement. Weeds and dock-leaves grew through the cracks. Then suddenly a clear loud voice said in my ear, "Look down among the dock leaves and you will find sixpence." I knelt down and felt around the green clumps, but nothing was there. Then I saw a clump growing almost out of the wall. I felt carefully around each leaf until at last I made contact with a silver sixpence. I fled with it to the Co-op and came home with a large bag of bacon pieces and a hock. That put a smile on my mother's face. With plenty of potatoes and root vegetables, we were assured of dinner for the next two days. Mum and Dad accepted the story I told them that I had found the sixpence. I was brought up to be honest but I couldn't tell them about the voice as well.'

Once again, Pauline was feeling responsible. The family needed money. It is not unlikely for the odd coin to be dropped and left lying on a well-worn path to the shops. Could the voice have simply been Pauline's way of getting the permission she felt she needed to look for it and to overcome the moral dilemma of keeping what she had found? On the other hand, she did find the money where she was told, so maybe Pauline has a fairy godmother after all. Fairy tales don't have to be about princesses going to cottages in the woods. They can equally apply to a worried little girl on her way to the Co-op for bacon scraps.

Cathy and her husband were missionaries in India for more than 20 years and lived in a large bungalow with very high ceilings in the Punjab. She wrote: 'One night I put our younger son to sleep in the corner of the bedroom. He was about two-years-old. I went back a short time later to see if he was asleep. He was but had crawled down to the end of the bed and was lying where his feet normally would have been. I moved him back with his head on the pillow and went out again. A little later I went in and found him with his head at the foot of the bed again and moved him back again. A few minutes later there was a tremendous crash. A cornice of the ceiling had fallen on his pillow. My son, however, was unhurt, as once again he had crawled down the bed.' Did some sixth sense warn Cathy's child that his normal sleep position was hazardous or were his repeated movements to the foot of the bed and the crashing ceiling merely separate events that coincided by sheer chance? Or did some friendly spirit or guardian angel protect him?

Ruth believes it was the voice of God that saved her baby boy's life. 'When my baby son Paul was six weeks old we were living in Godalming in Surrey. I had put him in his pram outside the back door in the spring sunshine and I was doing the washing-up in the kitchen with the back door open. Suddenly I heard a strange indefinable noise and went to investigate. Paul was frothing at the mouth and throwing himself around in the pram. I grabbed him and put him over my shoulder and patted his back, even hitting him quite hard, but he was arching his back and obviously couldn't breathe. I almost panicked. The nearest neighbours were too far away to hear even if they were in. So I knew only God could help me. I know that I spoke aloud: "God please help me – tell me what to do." Then I stood still and made myself keep calm. At that point the voice came to me and said : "Turn him upside down and hit him on the back." I know I said out loud: "Oh yes, of course. Thank you." I had to hit Paul twice really hard and then he gasped and breathed normally. I took him inside and sobbed: "Thank you, God," over and over again.'

To Ruth, a Quaker, it seems natural that the voice was that of God. But even people without a religious faith can believe in some higher form of intervention, whether it is fate or some force of nature or even that elusive but much desired commodity, luck. It could be argued that Ruth herself was projecting the voice she heard when blind panic was threatening to overwhelm her. She asked for help and then tried to be calm. That may have released enough mental capacity for her to reach the solution to her son's problem. What she took to be a voice could have been her own thoughts. But whatever the truth, the voice, whether projected or from God, was spot on in enabling her to save her son's life. Help does not always come in such a tangible form and afterwards it is hard to rationalise what happened except that an awful tragedy was averted.

A relationship with an adult that was supportive in life can, as far as the child is concerned, sometimes carry on. Perhaps this can be dismissed as the child's imperfect understanding of the real world or perhaps, in his ghost friends, he is merely externalising an inner truth that the dead can and do still influence us long after they are gone. Sheila's mother recalls: 'When my daughter was four or five, she was great friends with our neighbour, Mrs Tompkins. Mrs Tompkins was deaf, but she and Sheila had great conversations over the garden fence.

Mrs Tompkins, a Welshwoman, listened carefully to every clear, high-pitched word of Sheila's and Sheila listened to Aunty Tompkins. One day I had to tell Sheila that Aunty Tompkins had died. Sheila didn't cry, but looked a little dismayed. "I wish you hadn't told me mummy," she said, "I wouldn't have known." "But you would have to know sometime," I replied and she said, "No, because I still see her." "Do you mean with your eyes or your mind?" I asked. "With my eyes of course," said Sheila. "She's there in the garden." So I said, "That's all right, then, give her my love," and we left it at that. Then one night, Sheila woke up crying. "Tell Aunty Tompkins I love her, but not to stand too close to my bed. She frightens me." I said, "I'm sure she didn't mean to. Let's tell her." So we both said aloud, "Please Aunty Tompkins, we're pleased to see you, but don't wake Sheila so suddenly. You gave her a fright." After that we had no more problems. Aunty Tompkins stayed in the garden, except for two occasions when she appeared in Sheila's room. Then one night or early morning, Sheila called out to me, sobbing, "Aunty Tompkins came to see me. She said she's going now. She said goodbye. I'll never see her again." I didn't know what to say except, "I'm sure you will." But Sheila said firmly, "No, Aunty Tompkins told me goodbye and God Bless and that I wouldn't see her anymore." I told Sheila Aunty Tompkins must be with God now and we should be pleased for her.'

What is quite rare is the positive attitude Sheila's mother took, accepting the value of her daughter's experience and not feeling threatened by it or any need to disprove it. As it was, Sheila was able to work through the experience and let go at the appropriate moment.

Edna carried on a similar friendship. 'When I was little my parents kept a lock-up shop a mile from where we lived with my grandma. One afternoon, I decided to go along and join my mother there. When my mother saw me, amazed and shocked no doubt that a toddler had come so far alone, she asked, "Weren't you afraid to come all that way alone?" "Oh no," I replied, "I had Mr Taig (a friend of my parents who had recently died) and all my dead people with me."' Perhaps Edna's remarks were a bit of inspiration to get round the parental injunction 'you must never walk up the road on your own'. After all, Edna may well have reasoned, her mother could hardly check with the people concerned. In a world, however, where children are told stories about talking rabbits who wear clothes and are warned not to go out or the bogey-man will get them, it is not surprising the odd dead person pops up. Or, perhaps Mr Taig's spirit really was there and did make sure the little girl came to no harm.

Occasionally, however, it can be the children who become the helpful spirits, looking after their mothers. The anthropologist Margaret Mead, in *Growing up in New Guinea*, her study of the Manus tribe, says that in this culture it is the father who is the popular indulgent figure in the family and the mother is largely ignored by her children and indeed usually by her husband and his family as well. This situation will persist until the death of a male child, when the mother will assume the power of a medium with her dead child becoming her spirit guide. Margaret Mead recorded that little boys, who in life stuck out their tongues at their mothers, spat, sulked or struck out at any attempts to discipline them, become mother's little helpers in death. Their spirits communicate with a whistling noise (made through their mothers' lips) and these sounds can be interpreted by the mother in ways that give her a bit of authority in the family after all.

Death is a drastic way of changing the relationship between mother and son and fortunately there are easier ways of effecting a reconciliation during the inevitable quarrels of childhood. Sometimes fate can lend a helping hand. With Elizabeth, what seemed to be a sign from heaven helped her and her young son to form a better relationship. She was a single parent and problems came to a head after he had returned from a weekend with his father. 'He was very upset and stormed out of the room. I asked him if he wanted to talk. He said his father had gone on at him about being tied to his mother's apron strings and it made him feel very angry. He refused to talk about it as he said I wouldn't understand. It was getting dark but he said he was going out to think. Then he ran out, slamming the door. I came downstairs and sobbed into my hands, "Lord help me."

'Minutes later he returned with a book in his hands and I asked where he had got it from. He said he had found it open on the verandah of the cricket pavilion on the village green. It was the Alternative Service Book and was torn and burnt (obviously stolen and vandalised from the local church). The front page was torn out, but where it was burnt it opened at the words "But each of you must be quick to listen, slow to speak and slow to be angry". I asked him did he want to talk, but he just said he was tired and would appreciate a cup of tea. I went to bed that night thankful for what I believe was divine intervention and that my prayer was answered. Since that time life has been smoother for me and my young son.'

The discovery of the service book at exactly the right moment with a verse so appropriate to the stress of the conflict between mother and son seems so unlikely, that it is tempting to look for some external force, loading the dice in favour of a reconciliation. But it could also be argued that perhaps the cooling-off period for the son had helped to get the situation in perspective. Whether Elizabeth's belief in divine intervention is correct or whether a helping hand from her son's 'guardian angel' directed him to the cricket pavilion where advice was waiting, matters less than the fact that the experience did trigger off a change for the better.

Nellie was only sixteen, but her problems with her elder sister were long-standing. It is another fallacy that blood ties automatically mean love between siblings. Sometimes the best that can be hoped for is tolerance. Rarely is the one child the angel and the other all bad, but this is how it can seem to the children involved. Nellie's older sister had, she said, a biting tongue which on one particular occasion had driven Nellie to desperation. 'I was in a terrible state when I was suddenly conscious of a brilliant white light and such a comforting message given me by God. Of course, this was understood subjectively, but it was as real as any other voice. The experience really stuck. It was a moment of intense comfort to my injured feelings.' Afterwards Nellie was much more able to cope with her sister.

Helen Manning offers a psychological explanation for Nellie's experience. She thinks that the angel or light or vision was Nellie's way of personifying the good object as opposed to the sister who is 'bad'. After the experience the good and bad elements can become integrated in the sister, enabling Nellie to respond to her in a more positive way. Or perhaps when the odds are stacked against a younger child, a bit of divine intervention can help restore the balance, making her feel 'special and protected' and thus more confident to deal with problems.

Was it something from beyond or sheer luck that guided a lonely boy from his boarding school to find a substitute family? John is in his fifties now but remembers clearly how an overwhelming urge, seemingly from outside himself, forced him away from the piano practice which he was enjoying on a Sunday afternoon. 'I consciously set off for a walk in my favourite direction, but felt myself being urged and twisted around to walk in a quite unfamiliar direction. I remember feeling totally puzzled and a bit bewildered as I was literally forced through a strange copse on the school boundaries and along unfamiliar paths to the roadway. When I wanted to go along the road in one direction to the village where I knew the tuck shop would be open, I was forced to go the other way. Eventually I came to a cottage where a woman was clipping a hedge. It was a very hot day and I offered to help. The urge directing me ceased. Then she asked me in to tea. The warmth of the woman and her husband to a lonely small boy gave me much comfort. I went to see them practically every weekend after that, as my own parents could only manage to visit once a term and I came to regard her as a second mother.'

Psychic intervention can work in mysterious ways, sometimes leading a child into trouble although the situation may work out for the best in the end. June told me the story of her father, Oscar, who was born in India in 1877, the eldest child of an army chaplain. The family did not have much money and his wealthy Uncle Howard in England offered to educate Oscar on condition he could adopt the child who would take his name. Oscar's father's reaction was 'aren't we lucky' although his mother was in tears. But his father pointed out that they would not see Oscar for many years anyway, as he would have to be sent to England for his education. So Oscar and his mother, and the three younger children travelled to England to meet Uncle Howard. Then, on the appointed day, dressed in his Eton suit for the first time, Oscar took the train with his mother to Hastings where they were to meet Uncle Howard for lunch. Throughout the meal, the boy kept asking, 'Who are the men in the garden? Why are they wearing funny clothes?' Annoyed, Uncle Howard, sent for the gardener who said there was no one in the garden. Both the gardener and the waiter gave Oscar a funny look. Furious, Uncle Howard said that he was not taking on a boy who told lies. Then, as they were leaving the hotel, the waiter came up to Oscar's mother and said, 'Don't worry. He's got the sight. My father worked here before me and at one time there were prisoners of the Napoleonic wars tied against the wall. The clothes would have been like the boy described.'

The unexpected sight of the ghosts, although they may have made Oscar appear a liar in his uncle's eyes, saved him from a potentially disastrous relationship with a man obviously unsympathetic to children. Instead, Oscar's mother and the three children stayed with him in Oxford where he went to school and, although the family lived on the 'sniff of an oil-rag' as there were two households to maintain, they were very happy.

Eventually, however, Oscar's mother and the younger

children had to return to India. Oscar then became a boarder and often spent school holidays with another uncle in Yorkshire. He was unhappy there because the house was always cold. The day started with family prayers and Oscar should have been going down for them one morning when he saw the figure of a woman in a long dress going into his aunt's room. 'There must be plenty of time still if my aunt has not gone down yet,' he said to himself and, being a dreamy boy, he dawdled around upstairs. When he finally got downstairs, the whole household was gathered for prayer. 'I'm so sorry,' he said, 'but I just saw my aunt go into her room. I thought, as she was still upstairs, it was much earlier.' There was a hush. One of his cousin's kicked him and pulled him into his place. That afternoon, he was told off by his uncle for lying. But later another cousin told him that it was well-known that a figure haunted the house. Oscar saw her three times during the rest of his stay there. Again, a psychic incident made Oscar realise that another relationship with an uncle was not going to work either. He began spending more of his holiday time at the house of a friend's family who were more responsive to a dreamy small boy and enabled him to follow a more creative path in life.

Quite often the benevolent spirit is that of a grandparent. The Reverend Tom Willis, a Church of England priest with a great deal of experience of the paranormal told me: 'Grans drop back to see the latest addition. If you were dead and were a granny, wouldn't you want to come back to see the new baby? My wife, in her neat Irish way often says "I think the dead are closer to us than we are to them. After all they've been in both dimensions."

She doesn't know if she read it somewhere, or if it's her own idea, but I think it sums ghosts up pretty well. Granny will often keep an eye on the children. Children frequently report an old man or woman popping their head round the bedroom door at night. It is just the spirit of a grandparent lending a hand. There is nothing wrong in that. If granny were always following you around, it would be worrying, but if she is seen looking over the cot of the newborn, that's fine. Where a woman has lost her mother before her own child is born, it may even be wish-fulfilment.

'One mother I know was breastfeeding her new baby in the bedroom and her five-year-old was playing on the floor with his toy car. Suddenly the little boy looked up. "Grandad," he cried with delight. His mother looked up too and also saw her father who had recently died. Grandad appeared to walk downstairs and the little boy chased after him. Then he came back puzzled. "Where's grandad gone?" he asked.'

A rational explanation for a grandparent's reappearance could be that the child is confusing a memory with reality. Eileen Orford, a child psychotherapist at the Tavistock Clinic in London, commented: 'A gran who has died may be held in memory as someone who is very kind. So when a child is ill or unhappy, it is natural for him to revive the memory of a loving person to care for him.'

But could a child retain a memory of someone they never knew? Lindsay's mother found that she was sometimes pushed to give the demanding toddler enough attention. But it didn't matter because Lindsay had 'my other mummy'. 'I used to sit in my high chair and my other mummy used to come through the wall and sit by me,' she said. 'She would come through the wall in my bedroom and talk to me about all sorts of things and make me laugh. She looked very much like my mum, only she wasn't.' The identity of the 'other mummy' remained a mystery until at a family party, Lindsay caught sight of a pile of old family photos and pounced on one with delight. 'There she is – my other mummy.' It was her great-grandmother in an Edwardian wedding dress. She was almost the image of Lindsay's mother.

Lindsay's 'other mummy' always made her laugh. 'I sometimes thought she was nicer than my real mum.' No doubt the 'other mummy' never made unreasonable requests about cleaning teeth or not making a mess. She was never too tired or too busy or had a headache. She arrived when Lindsay was bathed and in bed and the miserable post-teatime rattiness from which most toddlers suffer had passed. No wonder she was such a cheery soul. By adulthood, this idealised person is on the whole relegated to fantasy, though there are people who go from spouse to spouse and family to family in search of perfection. Lindsay's 'other mummy' could have been a product of imaginative wish-fulfilment but the photograph raises questions that remain unanswered.

Elizabeth says her grandmother who died 21 months before she was born, used to pop in whenever she was sick as a child. 'I used to see the figure of an elderly lady, dressed in black and always wearing a little hat, approach my bed, sit looking at me for a few seconds and then seem to melt away into the shadows by the door. It didn't seem to worry me. I accepted it, though it certainly seemed to startle my mother and she used to say it was only my imagination or the results of a high temperature. But I knew the bedside visitor was my granny whom I had never met. The last time I saw her was when I was thirteen and was very ill with bronchitis.'

Grandmothers can be such strong figures in our lives that it is hard to say whether we conjure them up from outside or inside. Psychologists say that from childhood, our minds absorb authority figures – teachers, mothers, grandparents. Though we rebel against them occasionally, their voices go on in our heads and in times of stress, 'gran' can take over and we can almost hear her voice. Many middle-aged women still look furtively backwards when they go out if it looks like rain, almost hearing the voice of mother saying: 'Better take your mac, dear, you don't want to catch a chill.'

Children and teenagers psychologically need these nurturing figures. As I mentioned earlier in the chapter, it is very frightening, especially for younger children, that mum gets bad-tempered and even seems to hate them at times. So they tend to polarise things into fairy godmother and wicked witch. If mum's playing the wicked witch, then out comes the fairy grandmother to even up the score. Grandmothers are nearly always seen to be on the side of good and this is often hard to dispute when all a child knows of gran is her forever smiling face fixed behind a sheet of glass. Janet Boucher, a child psychiatrist says: 'Children know that granny existed even if they never met her. If she has died, then mum will usually speak of her in a nice way.' A grandmother can therefore, even if she is long-dead, become a vivid part of her grandchild's world, seeping into the child's consciousness and becoming his or her guardian angel.

But whether ghostly grandmothers are merely a powerful memory or real manifestations of the spirit world, they seem to serve a useful purpose as comforters of children. Although sometimes a ghostly grandparent can be frightening if the child does not know him or her or does not understand the purpose of the visit.

When Ann was three, she insisted she could see an old man standing across the road staring at the house. Her mother told her there was no one there, but the little girl was very distressed. Then, Ann said the old man was on their side of the road. Again her mother told her there was no one there, but Ann was still frightened. The next day, fearing that there might be a strange man lurking in the area, Jean, Ann's mother, asked her neighbours if they had seen anyone out of the ordinary. The little boy next door had told his mother that he had seen a man in his house and would not go to bed, but the mother had seen no one.

A few days later the same boy, in tears, told his mother that the man was at the front of the house. Ann told her mother the same, but if there was a man there, then only the children could see him. Ann then shouted from the garden that the old man was there. Her mother thought she looked frightened, but then she suddenly stopped being frightened and started running round the garden laughing as if she was being chased. Ann's mother began to wonder if the old man could be the ghost of her father, who had died just before Ann was born, and if Ann had been afraid of him until he actually came to play with her in their garden.

Rosemary was also frightened by the unexpected appearance of a grandparent: 'When I was very young, one of my aunties was taken very ill. I didn't know at the time, because she lived some distance away and my father had quarrelled with her. Then one night I awoke at about two o'clock. At the side of my bed was a little old lady. She didn't say anything, but just stood there. On the side of her head was a white mob cap. The only person I knew with a white mob cap was my granny, dad's mother, and she had been dead for several years. I was so frightened that I switched on the light and slept with it on all night. I didn't tell anyone because I didn't think they would believe me. Two years later, my aunt and my father patched up their differences and she told us about the time she was very ill in hospital. One night, so one of the nurses told her (my aunt was too ill to notice), a little old lady with a mob cap was sitting by her bed. The nurse later asked my aunt who the old lady could have been and my aunt said it was her mother.'

As far as Rosemary could tell this incident happened at about the same time as her grandmother had appeared in her bedroom. Could it have been that granny, knowing that her daughter was in trouble but that she and her brother were estranged, had gone to her grandaughter to try to tell her that her aunt needed help? Perhaps the old lady had hoped that Rosemary would tell her father about her dream and that this might prompt him to contact his sister.

Grandfathers too can be a source of wisdom and guidance. Laurence's grandfather was a very special person in his life and it seems that when he died, he came to reassure the lad. 'I was brought up with my grandparents. My grandfather had had a stroke and couldn't walk unaided. He used to go to the local bowling green in his wheelchair. When I was five, my mother remarried, but I remained with my grandparents till I was nine, when I moved in with my mother and her new family. I did this reluctantly because it meant leaving the people I had grown up with. Then when I had settled in the new house, I had a dream I was sitting at the top of the stairs with my grandfather standing next to me. A shape, which I now take to be a monk's habit with a hood, was moving up the stairs towards us. I said to my grandfather, "It's coming," but he said, "Don't worry. It's not coming for you." The next day, my stepfather broke the news that my grandfather had died in the night.'

Claire believes her grandfather first came back to her while she was a child and has continued to figure in her adult life. 'When I was nine, my grandfather, whom I loved very much, died. The night he died, he came to see me two hours after his death. At the time I didn't know he was dead and did not understand what he was saying to me, though now I do. Every time someone dies, he comes to tell me they are all right. When my daughter was very ill and we all thought she was going to die, he came to tell me not to worry. He told me she would get better and she did. I don't know how I would cope if he didn't come again.'

Grandmothers are often accused of spoiling grandchildren and leading them astray and according to Pamela, this can continue in the afterlife. 'When I was ten my gran died.' she said. 'The Grand National was her favourite horse race. She always had a little bet on it. The milkman used to put it on for her. The year after she died, she came to me in a dream and gave me the name of the horse that would win. I didn't say anything to anyone, but the horse won.'

It does not really matter whether helpful ghosts are an expression of something within the child or whether they really exist. As with children's imaginary friends (see Chapter 7), the advantage of a guardian angel or fairy godmother over a flesh and blood member of the family, is that he or she is unlikely to be too busy or concerned with personal affairs at a time of crisis.

9

Night Terrors and Phantom Foes

'My dad moved into my old room after he died and sleeps in the cupboard', said Emma. When we talked, Emma, the youngest of four children, was ten-and-a-half, slightly shy and mature for her age in many ways and a perfectly ordinary child but for her belief that the ghost of her father, who committed suicide, haunts the pleasant old-fashioned country cottage where she lives with her mother, Anna. 'I keep on feeling he is in my old room and sometimes I hear him,' she said. 'There was already something there. My friend who lived here before us, said her grandad was here. I can also feel my old dog Gus. Five months back, I told the dog, "Come back after you're dead so I can hug you." And he has come back.' He was her father's dog and did not long survive his master.

Is Emma's experience a case of the paranormal or a case for therapy? Neither the bustle of psychic investigators with their paraphernalia nor the probing of a psychiatrist seemed appropriate in this welcoming home.

'Emma has been quite confused since her father's death,' Anna told me. 'She thinks he is still around and can feel his presence. Emma was at school when his body was discovered. I brought her home, but she wanted to go straight back to school. My husband was very cold and undemonstrative with Emma. There was no relationship between them. I tried to foster close links, but the atmosphere was cold and repressive when Emma was little. I even tried holding back my affection in the hope he would take the initiative, but he went the other way. Emma would not even let him put her to bed, so great was the dislike between them.'

Eventually Anna told him that she could stand no more of his silences and coldness and asked for a divorce. But he just sat around the house and refused to speak. The day before he died the family had been planning to go on a Save-the-Whale walk organised by Greenpeace. Anna told her husband that she did not want him to come with them. He was not around when they set off, but that did not surprise her as he often used to go off for long periods without telling her. But he still wasn't around when they got back and Emma said, 'I bet Dad's run off or something.' Anna, thinking he had just gone off for a long walk told her not to be silly. The next morning she found his body in the garage. Soon after that Emma started saying that he had come back and was in her room.

Anna has since moved Emma into another room and redecorated her old one. At the moment it is occupied by Anna's eldest son and his fiancée, but that has not deterred Emma from believing her father still lives there. However, the strangest thing of all is that, unlike the cold, unfeeling father she remembers, Emma claims his ghost is warm and loving and gives her the affection which he never gave in life. Anna also admits to feeling her husband's presence in the house once and, like Emma, she found him warm, loving and comforting, something she said had become quite uncharacteristic of him, especially in the few days before his death which were particularly fraught.

These 'visits' of the surprisingly affectionate ghost of Emma's dead father seem to have begun after an uncanny incident at the Avebury Rings, stone circles just outside Marlborough in Wiltshire dating back to the Bronze Age. They are said to stand on a ley line, one of the straight lines which appear to connect ancient monuments and which many experts of the occult believe to be a source of great spiritual energy and power. Battered by the years and by locals, who have torn down the stones either for building materials or through fear of pagan powers they were said to possess, the remains of the Avebury Rings are less immediately impressive than Stonehenge. But in peaceful conditions they can be awe-inspiring.

When Anna and Emma visited them on Easter Monday 1989, the area was packed with tourists. Rosemary, a friend, told them to step inside one of the circles and see what they experienced. 'Avebury was very busy so I did not think I would feel anything,' said Anna. 'In the first circle, I felt quite light and good. I did not lean against any of the stones. Then we went over the road to the other circle. Immediately I was inside I felt an awful anxiety. I stood against one of the stones and felt my legs shaking. It was an awful physical and emotional experience. Emma was standing close to me. I wanted to get away so I stepped outside, leaving Emma still inside the circle.'

'In the first circle, I felt okay,' Emma told me. 'I didn't touch any of the stones. I felt at home like you do anywhere. Then we crossed the road to the second circle, where I stood against three big stones. They were about eight feet high. The first I stood against felt as though death was coming. I moved away quite quickly. I stepped across to the next stone and I felt like a swan flying. The third stone felt nice, but not too nice. Mum went out and I started feeling dizzy. Something not exactly dragged me, but called my name and drew me gently. I felt really sick and dizzy, so I ran out. "Come on," I shouted, "I want to go."'

Anna continued. 'Emma became very upset. She was crying, confused and wanted to run away. It was almost as if Emma linked into the family feeling, for her anger was just like the repressed anger of her dead father. "I'll never go there again," she cried.' Immediately afterwards, Anna says she felt her husband's presence in the house.

A child psychiatrist comments on parental suicide as the most adverse of situations a child has to face and that children often try to make sense of their grief by externalising it in some way. Whether by psychological or psychic means, the Avebury Rings brought out some of the conflict and pain surrounding Emma's father's death. In psychotherapy, there has to be the stage when a problem that has been repressed is brought out. This is not the healing stage – indeed it may lead to even greater apparent confusion, as it did in this case for Emma. But it opens the way to eventual acceptance, after which there can again be a way ahead. I told Emma that when my mother died in painful circumstances in contrast to her attitude, I coped with it by pretending she had never existed at all. If anybody mentioned her to me I changed the subject. I did this for about two years and then found that I did not need to do it any more. So one day, Emma might find that she does not need her father in her old bedroom any more and when that time comes she will know. She thought that seemed quite sensible.

In another case I came across, Edmund was going through a traumatic period with his father when he began to be haunted by a creature he called 'lion with glasses'. Edmund is now eleven and the lion's reign of terror covered eighteen months, from when he was about two-and-a-half until he was four. 'I remember the lion with glasses very well. He was in my bedroom in the big white house. I used to be sent to my bedroom while my first daddy was having his lunch. I saw the face on top of the curtains, hanging out looking over me, the lion with glasses. He was yellowy-brown and stared at me. I was very scared of him. He looked horribly at me as if he was going to jump out at me and kill me. I used to hide behind my wardrobe until someone came upstairs. He changed shape when people came so he wouldn't look so fierce. I knew he was real when I was small. I think now it was just the shape of the curtains. When the wind blew he looked bigger. He was only in that house, in that bedroom.

I used to dream about him. He was really awful, horrible in my dream. He used to peer in at my curtains. I used to try to get out of bed, but a force held me. He said, "You're going to die. I hate you for living in this house." I couldn't move. Now when I remember that, I think perhaps he was real. The force was holding me and the lion was talking. He had a horrible voice. He looked over me with his great glasses. He was just a head. Every night I had dreams about him. He was a very realistic lion. Sometimes when the wind was blowing, his face was twisted up. The last time I saw him was just before we moved. He said, "I'm going." He didn't follow us to the new house.'

Edmund's mother said, 'I can remember the "lion" almost as well as Edmund can. I had thought he arrived as soon as we moved to the south-west of England and into a white house with big rooms, high ceilings and ornate curtain rails. It was not a happy house. It was meant to be a new start after a separation. I was pregnant with my second child but my ex-husband found the noise and mess of a toddler difficult to cope with. I was trying to be good wife and mother and found the two conflicted. Edmund was shut in his room while my ex-husband ate lunch. He found family meals traumatic so it seemed less stressful to feed Edmund first.

'The "lion" was a real problem in our lives. We tried everything to get rid of it, asking it to go and even trying to drive it away, but it simply refused to get in the car! It was not until I left my husband and Edmund, the baby and I moved away to an old cottage in a market town about 20 miles away, that the lion went. Edmund told me that the lion had said he was leaving us. I thought we were the ones to leave the "lion". Perhaps we were both right.'

The family therapist Helen Manning comments: 'It must have been a fearful time for Edmund. Change was in the air with the arrival of the new baby and the parental relationship was rather tense and uncertain. There must have been increased uncertainty when he was sent to his room while his father had his meal, wondering what was going on during his absence? How does a child make sense of moving house, parental disharmony, a new baby etc. In some way maybe this "lion" was the expression of the threat and uncertainty Edmund was experiencing.'

Whether or not the lion was a psychic or psychological manifestation, at the time it was terrifyingly real for Edmund. Night terrors are a well-known childhood phenomena. Melanie Klein writes that at night, when invisible foes seem at their most potent, the child can feel hemmed in by all sorts of malevolent powers – sorcerers, witches, devils, phantastic figures and animals. The most important aspect of these night terrors would seem to be that, however improbable they might seem to adults, they should be treated seriously. A child should be able to confide in his or her parents without fear of being mocked or disbelieved. Sometimes the child must feel like the character in a horror movie who is being stalked by a nameless dread – a vampire or some such monster – and whom everyone refuses to believe until it is too late.

In the case of Ivy, she felt that she had to face her fears alone. 'When I was young I did not understand that everything was not normal,' she wrote. 'I think I would have been seven-years-old when I lived in sheer terror in our farmhouse. It was quite a lonely house, way up in the hills, directly on the Pennine Chain. I never told my parents what was happening because they would have said I was dreaming. But I'm now certain that the horrible, thin, wizened, toothless, spikey, grey-haired, ill-fed people were actually in my bedroom, which was built on to the Elizabethan part of an old farmhouse. They mocked and laughed and leered at me from behind the wardrobe and the wash stand and sometimes came close to my bed. I couldn't sleep properly and my mother bought me an iron tonic for she realised I had dark rings under my eyes.

'I was finally moved from my bedroom because my mother thought it might be too cold for me, but I have never forgotten those terrifying people. I actually lost weight. It was a kind of torment, as if something was trying to break me down. As a child, I had a feeling when the terror stopped of being the winner, as if I had conquered a kind of fear, something my mother and father could not do for me. Even at that early age, there was the knowledge that I must face it myself. That was 50 years ago and it gave me a lot of strength.'

The fears of a small child can be fixed in the strangest ways upon a particular place. Often the stairs seem to be especially frightening. When Sue was very small, she lived in Poole in Dorset and can remember feeling a presence on the landing whenever she went upstairs. 'It used to chase me down the stairs and I was terrified. It went on until my father painted the stairs white. They were originally varnished brown.' Beverley and her elder sister used to dash down the stairs because they felt there was someone behind them and Felicity told me that at times of tension in her childhood, she felt she could literally fly downstairs. Her parents were divorced when she was six, but before this, they lived in the country at Churchill, near Oxford.

'When I was very young,' she said, 'I used to stand at the top of the winding stairs and fly down. I used to count every step – there were 30. It happened in the evenings when I had been sent to bed. I was afraid of something upstairs and felt I had to get to the bottom. But I also had a tremendous feeling of power. I used to jump off the top step and land on my feet. The staircase was old and wind-ing with a thick rope instead of a bannister. I somehow got round the corner and touched the rope at one point in the middle. I never told anyone I was terrified at the top of the stairs. I knew it was going to happen as it happened most evenings. I also used to think there was something dark under the bed, a presence. My brother used to ter-rify me about a wolf. We used to have a *Peter and the Wolf* record and make ourselves listen to it. All this went on for years and finally ended when I was six when my parents divorced and I moved with my mother to a modern house in Cheltenham.'

During this period Felicity was also being troubled by a terrifying dream in which she thought she was drowning. This vanished when she moved house but she then began sleepwalking. 'Mum would find me by an open window or with my head in a drawer or at the top of the stairs, stand-ing quite still, though I was asleep. It was as if I was wait-ing for her to come and find me and wake me up and take me safely back to bed. I still sleepwalk occasionally.'

One explanation for night terrors given by psychol-ogists is that they might be 'eidetic images', pictures which are so vivid in a child's mind that he projects them into his surroundings like a cinema projector throws images on to a screen. Experiments have been carried out showing a child a picture and then removing it. Some children have the ability to point out details as though the absent picture was still there. It was said that between 30 and 90 per cent of children possessed this ability, though recent tests have put the figure as low as 7 per cent. Often the child cannot understand why the adult cannot see what he is seeing.

Is the child in some way taking pictures from his imagination, a book or a television programme and unconsciously projecting them against his bedroom wall at night? Would this explain the case of Jane who told me: 'When I was a small child of about two-and-a-half, we were living on a new council estate in Cardiff that had been built on a bombsite. I was lying in bed and I was convinced I could see a face on the wall – the same colour as the plaster, but with bright red lips. It was like the Queen's profile on a stamp or a cameo. I remember being absolutely terrified at the time of what the family refered to in later years as "my Lady Hoo-Hoo", which was what I must have called her when I tried to explain.'

But whatever the explanation of these externalised foes, there can be no doubt of their potency. Lucy, the third of four girls, used to wake up screaming from the age of about eighteen months. Jacky, her mother, can remember finding her cowering in her bed when she was about two, pointing at something across the room, wide-eyed with fear, but not having the words to express the cause of her terror. Once when she was a little older, Jacky found her pointing at the wardrobe, screaming, 'Lady, lady.' Jacky took her downstairs where a woman was reading the news on television. Lucy was so terrified by this that her parents had to turn off the television to stop her screaming. The night terrors persisted, but the only clue to their origin were her halting words about 'lady'. When she was three, Lucy would be found wandering about the landing, screaming and not knowing where she was going, eyes wide open. The next morning she had no recollection of this.

Shirley, now a medium, definitely blames her night terrors on the supernatural. She says that when she was little she was plagued by people in her bedroom – men, women and children – that no one else could see and would hide under her bedclothes with fear. Now she says she realises that it was the beginning of her psychic powers. She remembers when she was about five-years-old seeing an old lady with black robes sitting on her bed and an old man who used to stand in the corner. She was the middle child of five and used to frighten the others so much with her stories of these 'people', that eventually she was put in a bedroom on her own. Her mother used to get very cross with her for 'talking such nonsense' and smacked her so she learnt to keep quiet about what she saw. She says she now knows that her father was psychic, but he kept quiet about it then as her mother was a very dominant woman.

When Shirley was five, she told me that she used to sit on the step if her mother was out after about six o'clock, as she was too frightened to go in because of all the 'people' inside. She thinks it is sad if children do see things and like her do not have their fears explained. 'If you are afraid of your psychic awareness,' she said, 'your imagination will conjure up all sorts of horrid things.' With her own children, she has been very careful to protect them and show them there is nothing to be afraid of, while at the same time encouraging them to have lots of real friends and interests.

Teenagers' growing intellectual abilities do not necessarily make them less vulnerable to frightening experiences. The teenager knows more of the dark side of life than a young child, and yet no longer has the reassurance that 'wise' adults can put it all right. Gina was brought up in a household where her father was Muslim and mother Christian. She wrote: 'I remember in my early teens talking to God quite frequently because I was afraid of my parents as they often hit me. I found God was the only person I could ask for help and it was quite comforting to know or believe there was someone there to look after me. Though I think this belief led me to have contact with another power, for I started seeing presences in the house. Sometimes they shouted my name so piercingly that I became very afraid. I try to shut off the presences and shut off the voices and feelings, but it was all in vain. I couldn't contain these powers or force them to do anything for me or for anyone. I have written to clairvoyants and they have told me I have the gift which will develop. I have tried to tell my mother, but she just says, "Yes dear," and never takes it further. I feel I cannot talk to her about what happened, but I need to talk to someone.'

Gina's voices may well have represented underlying fears about her life in a mixed culture family, where she felt torn apart emotionally. But what is worrying about this story is that sensitive teenagers can be egged on by postal clairvoyants, some of whom may have no interest except in making money and can lead someone on without providing any support.

Graham an intelligent, very sensitive only child, says he became aware of his psychic powers after receiving spiritual healing for his asthma. 'I saw greens and purples and silver. I felt so tranquil. It was incredible.' Then the healer said to Sue, his mother. 'He's a very psychic child.' Since then Graham has been looking at things and perceiving things he hadn't seen before. He has begun to feel threatened by ghosts in his comfortable suburban home. 'One,' he said, 'was under the stairs and grabbed me. I was facing towards the main hall with my eyes shut and I felt him pull my shoulders and twist me. He pulled me. I think he must have been pulling me to face him. Another time, he tried to pull me into the cupboard. I saw him from the top of his forehead to the mouthline. He had a wispy beard, thin wire-framed glasses, a long nose and a kind face.' Graham perceives him as a scholar.

'One Friday recently, I was studying in my bedroom. Mum was at work. I glanced up at the door and saw a man standing there. As soon as I blinked, he was gone. He had a moustache, black beard and a Homburg hat with a black band. He wore a long woollen trench coat. Now when I'm in the house on my own and hear a creak on the stairs, I get really freaked out.'

Unlike Gina, Graham is not isolated with his fears. Although his father is away a great deal with his job and is not particularly enthusiastic about psychic matters, his mother is not only sympathetic but says she also feels the presences in the house. And other psychics also believe in these presences, some of whom have now taken on definite personalities – the scholar who stays under the stairs, the monk who gets hyped-up when Sue is hyped and rushes about yelling 'always busy, busy' and Graham's visitor in the homburg hat, perhaps checking up that Graham is studying.

I asked Graham, five months after I first spoke to him, what was happening to his ghosts and if he was still freaked out by them. 'Not since I've been going to psychic classes,' he said. 'I still see things out of the corner of my eye. I think I saw my grandad who recently died, but now it's all under control. I say a prayer when I go to bed and ask the four archangels to keep me safe. Then I visualise myself wrapped completely in a bandage, like a mummy, and I am safe until morning.'

To those who have not been haunted or have not felt the terror of being haunted, such precautions may seem like sprinkling magic dust to keep elephants out of your bedroom. But is our rational world any saner than Graham's? The French novelist, Romain Gary, once said that people were fools for thinking Don Quixote mad because he lived in a world populated by giants and ogres. It was Sancho Panza who was mad, he said, for not seeing that horror there really was in life.

10

Dealings with the Dark Side

I was lucky that despite his workload the Reverend Tom Willis, a Church of England vicar in Yorkshire, could spare some time to talk to me. As well as looking after two churches he is one of ten priests in the diocese of York who have been appointed to deal with cases of occult disturbances. 'The old word for us is exorcists, but I don't like using that word as it conjures up an image of black cloaks and flames coming out of my fingers,' he said. Married with five children, he has been involved with the paranormal for more than 20 years. 'There were a lot of problems in the 1960s. People thought I was a nut when I said that the occult was a growing problem. Then the flood came and the Samaritans started to ring up the C of E regularly, asking for help. I didn't have much experience, but I was thrown into the front line. I used to go out with the Samaritans and I also used to get called out by the police.'

I asked him if he believed that in this day and age evil

spirits could possess young children. 'If people themselves believe they are possessed, then it may well be a
psychological case. But some people do seem to have evil
around them and may display weird behaviour,' he replied. 'I know a Roman Catholic priest, a down-to-earth,
likeable, Irish, beer-drinking priest, who was called to a
case of possession in a teenager. He was very dubious till
he saw her lying rigid and then taking off four or five
inches from the floor. He realised something serious was
going on and commanded the evil to depart.'

We went on to discuss whether he thought evil was a
real living force that could think and act. 'There is a fascination with evil at a subconscious level. No one talks
about the possibility that evil may have intelligence. It is
considered twee – like believing in fairies – to regard evil
in that way. But the minute war is gone from one part of
the planet, it pops up in another. A disease, too, is erad-
icated but another rapidly takes its place. Evil is a blob
that you clear from one place and it appears in another.
The problem in dealing with the occult is that you will
have preconceptions according to whether you believe in
the spiritual or not.'

He agreed that children were possibly more psychic
than adults. 'They lose this power as they get older. I suppose it's because logical processes take over, but I don't
really know.' He also warns strongly against dabbling
with the occult for fear that what is called up might not be
what was asked for. The ouija board, he told me, has a
strong fascination for children. 'I speak to children in
secondary schools and warn them off the ouija board. I
recently asked 100 fourth and fifth year kids, fourteen and
fifteen year olds, how many of them had played with ouija

boards. Two-thirds put up their hands, there were less girls than boys. The girls were more interested in the astrological side. The teacher gasped at the sea of hands that went up. It is partly a craze of that particular age group.'

Before speaking to the Reverend Willis, I had already been told about the dramatic and horrifying effects of the ouija board on an impressionable child's mind. A few days before a mother had told me that when her daughter was about twelve, she and some of her friends had been playing with a ouija board in the school cloakroom at lunchtime, after they found a book about it in the school library. The daughter believes she picked up a spirit because she then started to be haunted by an oldish man. 'He used to sit on her dressing table,' said Pat, the mother. 'He followed her all the time. He used to just sit there watching her. It was horrifying.' Things got so bad one night when Pat's husband was at work, that Pat rang their Catholic priest, but he was out. 'My daughter was completely hysterical. I talked to her to calm her and we sprinkled holy water round her room. After that, it seemed to quieten down. I made her promise never to fool around with a ouija board again.'

Said the Reverend Willis: 'The ouija board will give accurate information at first and after a while the participants get fascinated. A spirit may claim to be a cavalier killed in the civil war and come out with lots of facts. After four or five weeks, there will be several foolscap sheets of facts about a battle, which when they are checked at the local library prove to be entirely accurate. The ouija board users then think they have got a tame cavalier. But soon messages start coming like "Tell Jack he will die in three weeks time" or "Your wife is having an affair with your brother". The spirit, who apparently told the truth for the first six weeks he was around, is now creating havoc and confusion with his warnings of death and deceit. Both the Jewish and Christian faiths warn people not to dabble. The spirit seems nice and friendly at first, then begins to feed the destruction. One favourite ouija board remark is "You will have an accident at Christmas". So the bloke who has received the message says, "Right I won't go out at Christmas," and stays in on Christmas day. At midnight on Boxing Day, he heaves a sigh of relief, till someone says, "But there are twelve days of Christmas." So he makes it through and hangs on till January 5th before going out. But then he starts wondering, "Which Christmas did it mean?" So there is always the fear hanging over him.'

The activities of poltergeists, the noisy ghosts who are alleged to cause so much disruption in houses, are also often linked with children.* But whether these are spirits which enter homes from beyond or manifestations created by the disturbed state of mind of one of the occupants of the house is open to debate. 'The current theory on poltergeists is that some electrical force comes from a living person who is repressing great anger,' the Reverend Willis told me. 'From one, I got the biggest electric shock I have had in my life. It knocked me off my feet. The force then went through the fifteen-year-old son of the family I was visiting, but although it had been lessened by passing through me, he still crumpled up. By the time it reached the mother, she still felt enough to

---

* This is borne out by accounts of various phenomena in *Poltergeists*, by Alan Gauld and A. D. Cornell, Routledge and Kegan Paul, 1979.

say, "Ouch what was that?"

'At the moment I've got four poltergeists on the go. There's a sudden run on them. I had none in the previous three months. In one of the worst cases, a woman had been dabbling in Satanism. She had given it up, but not renounced it. She had her kids baptised and they brought home the baptism candles. The candlesticks flew across the room and things started to happen. I was called in and I found it could read my mind.

'I have had objects flying about while I stood in the midst. I had read about this, but never believed it till I saw it. In one house, there was a dog ornament on the mantelpiece where objects kept moving. Suddenly, it seemed to fly across the room. "The dog's gone again," said the householder. I was sitting there and heard a clunk in the kitchen. All the doors were closed. "Don't move," I said and I went into the kitchen. There was the dog ornament on the floor. It had gone clean through the living-room wall. I consulted a physicist at Hull University. "Is it possible for objects to move through brick walls?" I asked him. "According to the quantum mechanical tunnel theory, if it went at the speed of light, there would be no problem. But it's not proveable since you can't hurl objects at the speed of light!" he said.'

Poltergeist activity can be less spectacular but still frightening for those involved. Jill, now married and with a family of her own, told me this incident from her childhood: 'I was always scared of the back bedroom where I used to sleep. We moved to the house when I was eleven. The main thing I noticed was that it was always freezing in there. I had a friend to stay not long after we moved. We had single beds quite a way apart. I woke up in the night and my bed was shaking. I got up and it carried on shaking. My friend woke up too and her bed was shaking. I told my parents and they said, "It's because we live near the railway." But we were about half a mile from the track which was on the other side of the house. It was the only time it happened in the six years we were at the house. It never happened in my friend's house and she lived next door.

'Later, I started to have a dream about an upside down cross. We weren't a religious family and never went to church. I was horrified to be told by my friends that it was to do with the devil. Not long after I had an awful vision of the devil. He had huge horns like a ram and a horrible face. His face was dark and half-ram, half-human. I think I said a prayer and I felt a physical force was trying to crush me. I was absolutely terrified. It lasted 10 or 15 seconds I suppose, but it was like eternity. My parents took no notice. They always said it was my imagination. They were strong people who didn't show emotion.'

There have been cases of poltergeist phenomena being produced by blatant fraud. Dr Hans Bender, a German parapsychologist, videotaped a little girl, supposedly the victim of poltergeist activity, leaping out of bed, slinging an ornament, hopping back into bed and shouting 'Help, mummy'. But most cases are not funny.

High profile cases such as the Enfield Poltergeist have been well documented.[*] The manifestations which began in a council house in north London in August 1977, involved a mother, separated from her husband, and her children. Rose, the eldest, was thirteen, Janet, around

---

[*] See for example *This House is Haunted*, by Guy Playfair, Sphere Books, 1981.

whom the activity seemed to centre, was eleven, Pete was ten and Jimmy, the youngest, was seven. The activity lasted for more than 14 months. By the tenth day the *Daily Mirror* newspaper had been called in along with a full-time investigator and before long the house was like a television studio. There was also a whole host of regular visitors, each with their own psychic axe to grind. Almost every conceivable type of psychic phenomena appeared – furniture was overturned, a growling man's voice spoke through Janet, messages were left on the bathroom wall, paper and cloth were charred, apparently from sponta-neous combustion and there was spoon-bending, lev-itation by Janet, flying Lego bricks that struck a photo-grapher although no one seemed to hurl them and the girls being thrown out of bed.

The poltergeist's activities wound down around Christmas and it did not carry out its threat to eat up all the chocolates. This was fortunate as Guy Playfair, one of the psychic investigators, had bought a large box for the Christmas tree and had promised the children that they could have them if the box survived until Christmas. Eventually the poltergeist activities ceased as mysteriously as they had begun. Throughout the period, Maurice Grose, the other main psychic investigator, kept in touch with the family, helping both with their practical and emotional problems and this may well have con-tributed, as much as anything, to their return to normal-ity.

Less spectacular but more disturbing, to my mind, is the case of an eight-year-old boy, Kenny, who was re-jected by his foster-parents because he was blamed for bringing a poltergeist upon them. Kenny's foster mother suffered from a progressive illness and he had been diagnosed as educationally backward, which is sometimes regarded as a significant factor in poltergeist cases (or it may be that so-called retarded children are less able to explain what really happened). There was considerable disturbance in the house – bookcases spilling and china smashed. A medium was called in and identified the presence of a boy called Don who said he played with Kenny in the garden. The foster father said that Kenny often told him he was playing with a boy called Don who had a bicycle, when in fact there was apparently no one there with Kenny (though as we have seen an imaginary friend is not at all unusual). This Don was linked by the medium with a young down-and-out who had died in the area.

A newspaper reporter did point out at the time that there was a real Don with a bicycle who lived nearby, whom Kenny sometimes played with. But this was ignored and by the time the police and priests had said their say and the neighbours had offered their words of wisdom, it was only left for the friendly neighbourhood self-styled white witch to bring the situation to boiling point by pinpointing 'the malevolent force' to the unfortunate Kenny. This force had entered Kenny apparently because of some unspecified early trauma in his life. She felt that if he was removed everything would be fine. So the lad was sent to new foster parents and the activity ceased (though apparently nothing occured at his new home).

Whatever the psychic truth of events, it seems a sad indictment that it should be the child, perhaps most in need of help, who was seen as the cause and was the one to suffer. It is perhaps dangerous to view a child's psychic experiences, bad or otherwise, as emanating from the child in isolation. They are a part of the whole family situation and the removal of one member is perhaps a false and particularly sad solution. Peter King, president of the Reading National Spiritualist Church considers that in Kenny's case the medium could not have been a responsible one or she would have tried to enlist the help of the spirits and talk to the poltergeist.

Sometimes, it would seem, the poltergeist is not malevolent, but unhappy and taking out his feelings on the more vulnerable members of the family, the children. Lilian, a psychic counsellor, told me about a family with four children, who believed they were being persecuted by a poltergeist. The mother, a nurse, insisted that their house was haunted by a small thing which was quite vicious, though the creature was not malevolent to her personally. Her husband knew of the presence, but believed that the less said about these matters the better. Two of the children, the eldest and the youngest, were terrified of the creature and would not sleep in a particular bedroom because they said it was there. Lilian says that when she went to the house, she felt the presence was eluding her. She stayed in the bedroom with it, but it went off into a corner. However, as Lilian began chatting to the mother, she says she felt the small thing attach itself to the woman – 'It seemed to be a small boy who could neither see, hear, nor speak and its only anchor of security was the mother'. Lilian asked the mother if she had ever known a child like that. The mother immediately recognised it as her sister's child who had lived in the house and slept in the bedroom her children were now afraid of. Her sister had shown this child very little affection and it had been left to her alone to show him love and warmth. The child had died when he was about two. Lilian said this child was jealous of the children, his cousins, living in the house and usurping 'his mum' by taking up her attention.

Lilian tried to contact the spirit of her own dead mother to come and look after the child. But Lilian's mother was out of reach and the ghost child was determined to stay. Eventually Lilian said, 'Look I can't get rid of it for you, but now you know who it is, do you really want it to go?' The mother decided 'no' and the little deaf, dumb and blind spirit remained in residence, but proved much more co-operative from then on.

Jealousy was also a factor with the young female poltergeist who frightened Moira and attacked her sister. In this case, the family moved on after many years of haunting. The poltergeist was alleged to be one of grandad's old flames from the war who got very annoyed with anyone else getting his attention, even his grandaughters of whom he was very fond.

Moira told how when she was four, she, her baby sister and mum and dad moved to a big old house which they shared with their grandparents. 'Even then I sensed something strange about the house and used to lie awake at night listening to the strange noises from the landing. I used to cry because of the sounds outside my door. But no one ever appeared. Then when I was about seven, the noises got too close for comfort and I locked myself in the toilet for about two hours, till mum came and took me on a tour of the house to prove that nothing was there. One night, when I had just started secondary school, I was sitting on the floor in my grandad's lounge when suddenly a wall light switched itself off and then on and off again. My grandad, who was there with me, just laughed and said, "She's here again." Then he told me he had recently been seeing a young girl of about twenty walking behind him. Sometimes, he said, she was just a white outline and at other times she looked like flesh and blood. I pressured him for more details, but he wouldn't talk about her much. I am certain no one else knew.

'Then when my sister was eleven, she woke up scream-ing one night. She said a girl had come into her room, hurt her and then rushed into my room. One night soon after that, I woke up and couldn't get back to sleep. Some-one was walking up the stairs. I began to panic – burglar-ies were common in our area – something moved across to my sister's room and I heard paper being thrown everywhere, then the books. I thought she must be sleep-walking. I screamed to mum but when she went into Lor-na's room everything was in its place.

'A couple of months later, my mum, sister and I moved out, as my parents had agreed to a divorce. We moved into a flat and my grandparents sold the house. A medium later told my grandad that the poltergeist was a young woman who had nursed him when he was injured during the war and had fallen for him.'

Once Moira discovered her grandad's ghost, it ex-plained her own earlier 'spooky experiences'. The 'girl' who attacked her sister fitted in, as did the apparent ran-sacking of her sister's room. Not long after, the family split up, which would suggest that there was great under-lying tension there. Did the family members, involved in the marital upheaval that could well have been simmer-ing for years, need a poltergeist to make sense of the tensions and stresses they must have felt? Or was this simply a haunting that fitted in with the medium's explanation of the 'young nurse' still pining after her lost love and jealous of the affection the old man showed to his little grandaughters?

A strong Christian faith cannot always provide protection against apparent manifestations of evil. In fact, it may be that it provides an even more tempting target for such forces. Andrea wrote: 'When I was sixteen, I had an experience during Lent. Being the regular church organist and piano player, I was asked to play for four consecutive Tuesday evenings. On the second, before starting the service, I sat at the piano rehearsing a few hymns with the congregation in the church hall, where the service was being held. While practising the last hymn, I casually peered over to the front doors – I presume I was expecting to see any late arrivals – but a kind of woman was staring in at me, expressionless with no features. She had dead, white flesh with a black scarf of some kind that went all round her head. I went dizzy and my heart started beating faster, but I just couldn't tear my eyes away from it. I looked away but had to look again and finally I let out a loud gasp. Everyone suddenly stopped singing and the vicar asked what was wrong. For some unknown reason, I said I thought I'd seen my dead grandmother. Why I said that I don't know, but what I'd seen was unexplainable. The vicar's wife came over to comfort me and said that it was probably Satan, who sometimes tries to destroy church services and that my playing the piano had made me a target.'

Whether Andrea did see the devil or a manifestation of her own fears of being possessed, we do not know. Perhaps, poltergeists and demons say something about the fears of a growing child and indeed his or her whole family? Perhaps we think we see demons or are being attacked by poltergeists, when we are actually saying 'I feel attacked by tensions going on around me'. The phenomena of poltergeists and possession appear to need deeper study than is currently provided by psychic investigators and the media. Meanwhile, on the positive side, Eileen Orford of the Tavistock Clinic, says, 'We need ways of thinking about our fears. They are better in the form of monsters than left lying in the unconscious. At least as monsters they are not a nameless dread.'

Changelings and Witches

Nothing seems more innocent and beautiful than a sleeping new-born child. But imagine if you were to pick up that child and it suddenly opened its eyes, smiled to reveal a full row of teeth and said, 'I am very small but my teeth are very sharp.' That scenario – so terrifying because of the contrast between innocence and malevolence – occurs in John Steinbeck's novel, *The Long Valley* and introduces a character to be found in folklore all over Europe – the changeling.

The legends describe the changeling as a wizened, misshapened baby, hairy and with a monstrous head, which is left in the cradle as a substitute for a human child snatched by the fairies or underground elves. It is said to eat ravenously but never grow (or if it grows, to be horribly deformed) and to cry continously. The fairies or sprites are said to desire human babies for their tender flesh and to carry them off to fairyland where they are made much of.

Folklore offers various remedies to make the ever-crying changeling laugh or to trick it into revealing its true age. The story of the soldier and the egg exists in various versions in many parts of the country, but basically it is about a soldier who returns home from the wars to find his younger brother still in the cradle after some 20 years. The mother has not caught on yet that there's anything amiss 'He's still a growing lad, dear' she says, but the soldier has knocked around a bit and has his suspicions. He empties an eggshell, fills it with water and begins heating it over a fire which amuses the changeling enough for it to laugh out loud and say, 'Old, old I am, but in all my years I have never seen a soldier brewing beer in an eggshell.' The deception now revealed, the soldier feels free to attack the changeling with a whip and, by magic, it vanishes and the long lost brother, now a grown man, is restored to the family. According to some versions he is a little peeved at the reunion because in fairyland, where he had been imprisoned for all those years, he lived the life of Reilly and knows that conditions at home might be a little more basic. Other versions of the tale neglect the egg brewing and go straight into the whipping option at which point the fairy or elf who carried out the substitution appears, crying, 'Do not attack my child for I never did yours any harm,' and returns the missing baby. Victor Hugo used a variant of the changeling legend in *The Hunchback of Notre Dame*, where the baby Quasimodo, the hideous but immensely strong cripple, is swapped for the beautiful Esmeralda. But here the substitution is carried out by gypsies not fairies.

As the changeling is so widespread in folklore, it is interesting to speculate on what basis there could be for it in reality. Was it the way for parents in less enlightened times than ours to come to terms with deformed or handicapped children? I asked a doctor with an interest in paranormal experiences about the medical aspects. 'The description of a changeling is not identifiable as a particular syndrome,' he said, 'rather a series of deformities that separately or together would mark a child as odd. There are children who look odd from the moment they are born and come to look stranger. When parents have a child that looks strange, one acceptable hypothesis in times past was that the devil had got into the child somehow. Many conditions – cretinism or gargoylism for example – can give rise to a bizarre and unattractive appearance. Dietary shortages in times past can explain much of the lack of growth, especially in poor families. A large head can of course be linked in some cases with hydrocephalus. In those days, a high proportion of children failed to thrive and infant mortality was as high as 50 to 60 per cent. The changeling explanation was a convenient explanation for unfortunate parents who produced a 'monster' and made it more acceptable to them. Until the last 50 or 60 years, most unpleasing looking children died. Only strong healthy children survived.'

For the child taken to be a changeling, life could be rough, especially if the parents decided to use the whipping method. In 1843, *The West Briton* newspaper reported the case of a J Trevelyan of Penzance who was charged with ill-treating one of his children. The child was said to have been regularly beaten by the parents and the servants and from fifteen months old had been left to live outside. The parents' defence was that he was not their child but a changeling and the case against them was dismissed.* 'You have to remember that a century and a half ago,' said my doctor friend, 'the railway had only just broken through to Cornwall and until then it had been virtually cut off from the rest of the country. When Wesley went there in the 1780s he found a land rife with paganism and folklore. Cornwall at that time was appallingly backward with gross poverty, great ignorance and conditions that horrified Wesley.'

Times may have improved but the problem lingers of the child who does not quite fit in with the family, the 'Cinderella' who can be of either sex. 'As a doctor,' my friend continued, 'one sees women who do not like one of their children and feel very guilty about this. In the past, the hypothesis that the Devil was in the child made it easier for them to accept this situation. When people used to have a number of children, anything up to a dozen, this was not uncommon – the unloved child who was blamed for everything.'

The past sixty years have seen the growth of the social services in Britain, which give support to the parents of handicapped children and the myth of the changeling, which could have provided an excuse for mistreating or neglecting a child, has faded (although child cruelty, sadly, continues). But if one old belief has retreated, another surrounding children has managed to grow in strength – possession by demonic forces. Perhaps the flames of this belief have been fanned by films like *The Exorcist* (child possession), *Rosemary's Baby* (a child sired by Satan), *The Omen* (a changeling) and all the B-Movies that followed, trying to cash in on the vogue for tales of

* This case is quoted in *The Folklore of Cornwall* by Tony Deane and Tony Shaw, Batsford, 1975.

Satanic children. In one disturbing film, based on Ray Bradbury's story, *The Baby*, a baby is born with a mature mind and murderously attacks its parents for daring to bring it into the world away from the peace and quiet of the womb.

Despite such films and stories it is fairly safe to assume that babies are innocent, although, in the eyes of the Church, we are all born in the state of original sin. The Reverend Christopher Armstrong, chaplain to the Archbishop of York, told me: 'The official Church of England position is that children are not born innocent, but in original sin that we all have to bear,' he said. 'In baptism the child is incorporated into Church, but this does not give total immunity against sin.'

I then asked him about the problem of possession and how the Church of England in the late twentieth century dealt with it. 'All bishops now appoint an official exorcist in each diocese to help contain the more hysterical forms of possession. It is not common but most priests will have come across cases where it is believed by the people involved that a child or adult is "possessed". The parish priest will make an initial investigation himself with prayer, but if he can't cope, he will then call in the specialist help of the official exorcist, who will have had additional training. Initially, the exorcist will look at the whole situation to try to find out the real meaning of the apparent possession. There is usually a big overlap between the psychological, psychiatric and exorcism aspects. We are concerned with a muddy area that remains muddy when everyone has had their say, though there is much work being done in the church at the moment to try to clarify this.

'The Church has got to address itself to the problems of evil, even today. One problem is media exaggeration. The great problem for churches can be seen if you go into any Smith's bookshop. There will only be a small shelf for religious publications, but the occult section is growing all the time. With the recession of Christian values, there is a need for something to satisfy people's concern with the spiritual side of life and some may turn to more bizarre and dangerous expressions for the other side of reality.

'In some areas, people are likely to ring the police or their GP when they come against problems of this kind. The doctor has very much taken over the priest's role in the High Street. If the doctor has a good relationship with the clergy, he may direct troubled people to the church. In a few cases, a person may be possessed in some way. I am very uneasy about using the words demons or Satan, because of the dramatic overtones they conjure up. But we know that there are powers of evil as well as of good and in some cases people will be imbued with evil rather than good. In some cases a blessing ceremony can help. But it needs to be more than a simple blessing. It needs to involve prayer and the laying on of hands, which is a biblical form of healing. In fact, the emphasis should be very much on healing rather than casting out and what is cast out, should be replaced with something new. There is a parable in the bible about Jesus casting out demons from a house. The house was cleaned but nothing was put in the place of what had been taken out, so the demons came back and brought their friends. Because this sort of healing takes a Christian form, by implication, there is a new way forward through the body of Christ.'

David Murphy of the Catholic Truth Society says that while the official Catholic view is that it is theoretically possible for the devil to enter a person, in practice no one would ever be permitted to exorcise without careful scrutiny. An exorcism would be conceived very cautiously and the Church would look at other levels of explanation for the problem.

Hollywood has conditioned us to think of possession in terms of spectacular special effects. However it can be more subtle in real life, although none the less unnerving for the parent who believes that his or her child may be possessed. When I discussed Louise's story with her, she struck me as a very pleasant, rational woman. She feared that her son Edmund had been possessed even before his birth. She believes this 'thing' entered Edmund in Cornwall where he was conceived. 'I had an overwhelming desire to go to Cornwall for most of my childhood and adult life. I believe that the "being" somehow got me to Cornwall so it could be born again through my son. The year before Edmund was conceived, we were staying on the south-west side of Bodmin Moor, camping beside a river bank, when I experienced an overwhelming desire to walk along the river bank early in the morning. I thought I saw lots of figures – not as distinct people but as indistinct shadows – lots of figures, maybe a hundred. I felt as if they were standing along the banks of the river welcoming me.'

At the time Louise contacted me, in 1989, Edmund was eight. 'From the beginning, he was always very different. Sometimes I would look at him and it was as if his face was not his face any more. During my elder son's pregnancy and birth I felt calm and happy. But Edmund's pregnancy was very different. All I remember about it is feeling thoroughly exhausted and physically ill. I also felt very depressed and worried – though I felt it was inevitable he would be born. It was as though he had to come.'

Louise believes that a message from Edmund altered her carefully laid birth plans. It was agreed by the midwife that Louise should give birth in a squatting position. All was going well till the final examination in labour. 'Suddenly I felt taken over, that I had lost the power to be me. I felt the child and had to lie prone. The midwife and Tony, my husband, tried to haul me up the bed so I could squat as I had planned, but I felt I had to refuse. It was not like with Harry, my elder son. I felt I had no choice. Then when Edmund was born, the cord was wound tightly around his neck. The midwife told me if I had given birth in any other position except prone, he would most likely have died.'

After Edmund's birth everything that could, went wrong. Illness meant her husband could not work for a long time and problems with their house had them camping in one room. 'I felt so swept along and taken over. Somehow in some way, I've always felt that Edmund had a will so strong that any desires of mine or anyone else's would be overridden. Could that will have manifested itself even then? From the first he was a very difficult baby and his eyes were peculiar. They seemed unlike a baby's eyes. I remember sitting up in bed with him just after he was born. He was propped up on my knees and he gazed around the room very slowly and calmly. Calculating is the way I've always described it, but how can a baby of only a few hours look calculating? I phoned my mother soon afterwards. I wanted to say "Help, I've had a strange baby," but I didn't because I could never have explained why I found him strange. Edmund looked like a little old man when he was born. People would say you wouldn't know he was a child.'

Louise was very ill and her husband had to take on a lot of the caring for Edmund during the next few years. 'Edmund would easily become what we described as "hyped-up", which could be generated by a number of things including some foods, watching television or a computer screen, over-excitement or some kinds of fluorescent lighting. He would seem physically changed as if his body had become like an old man's. His skin felt strange in these moods, not firm like a child's and would go yellowy-white in colour. His voice would become loud and strident and he'd use foul abusive language. He would make a hideous face (which always reminded me of a gargoyle) and scrunch his hands up and hold them rigidly beside his ears. His eyes would roll up and he would leer. It always made me feel terrible and I couldn't fathom why he was behaving like this. If people didn't like him, he became worried and reacted badly. He would react badly to a person or situation that made him feel rejected. The more people he was with the more likely he was to lose control.'

She described Edmund as a gifted child with a high IQ, but having many problems with conventional schooling. At eight, he was asked to leave the private school he had been attending for only a few weeks, because of his disruptive behaviour – 'an evil feeling or presence which Edmund seemed to bring into the class' was how an overwrought teacher described it.

A friend then suggested Louise might take Edmund to

a psychic healer he knew. 'The healer felt that Edmund was possessed by an evil spirit,' said Louise, 'and suddenly everything fitted together. "What does it look like? How does it manifest itself?" I asked. "I see it sitting on his shoulder," the healer said and made the face I had seen on Edmund when he was "hyped-up" and had almost seemed possessed, many times in the past. "It's quite a malevolent sort of chap," the healer continued, who's making Edmund unhappy and doesn't want to go off where he belongs." But she reckoned she could get rid of it for us. At the actual healing, my husband, the healer and I made a circle and the healer talked to the spirit, telling it that it was in the wrong place. "The time has come for you to go on," she said. I felt tremendous relief and tears rolled down my cheeks. My husband felt really drained. We didn't see anything and Edmund didn't feel anything in the next room where he was playing. We just felt very drained. But since then, we have never seen Edmund's strange face and there has been a dramatic change in his behaviour. The treatment has had a profoundly calming effect on him.

'We had several more treatments with the healer as she wanted to work on my relationship with Edmund and also on him through me. She thought that Edmund had other "companions", who were not so closely linked and certainly not malevolent but who ought to be removed. Edmund often wanted me to be there during his treatments and at first I saw nothing. But on one occasion, I was amazed to see a misty semi-transparent film or sheet lifting itself off his body and forming into a very tall indistinct shape beside him before vanishing, all in a few seconds. I felt a sense of regret and sadness emanating from this figure. When the treatment finished, Edmund just got up and ran off to play as if nothing had happened. I ached with sorrow for my son until recently. But the change in him since the healing has been amazing. During the last school holidays, for the first time, he went to a holiday club at the local gymnasium with a whole range of activities and seemed to be enjoying it and coping fine.'

Whatever happened at the healer's, it was obviously some sort of trigger. Helen Manning, the family therapist, agrees that there are similarities between this kind of experience and therapeutic practice. 'Any form of psychotherapy raises the individual's awareness and gives credibility, acknowledging the experience and giving value to what is said and felt. Afterwards it is different. Awareness is raised and things can't be the same. If you acknowledge the experience, whether the child's or mother's, it enables them to make a change. It need only be something small. Exorcism is like this.'

My doctor friend commented: 'One of the great functions of all healers is to pronounce something and let people off the hook. Miracles are a fascinating subject, though they upset many rationalist doctors. If people are trapped in a disturbed and disturbing relationship and an immense authority can say, "I have removed the devil, now you may love your child," sometimes there is a breakthrough in the relationship.'

Perhaps the early traumas of Edmund's life, Louise's illness, the stress surrounding his pregnancy and his 'differentness' all contributed to some breakdown in relationships, which the healing repaired. Or it may be argued that Edmund was possessed by some spirit in

Cornwall at his conception, as Louise, an intelligent, articulate woman, who is now studying for a degree in science, believes. Whichever theory is correct, the experience with the healer triggered off a dramatic improvement.

It is a fallacy that all mothers fall instantly in love with their babies. If the birth was difficult or the circumstances at home are not ideal, it is not surprising mother love can be slow to grow. But this can result in tremendous guilt and anxiety, which can be passed on to the baby, making him or her difficult to feed and frequently sick. Then this, in turn, can make the mother feel even more inadequate and depressed.

The case of Judy is interesting, because the supernatural force she encountered did not turn her against the baby but helped her to love it. 'I was just twenty with a four-month-old baby,' she wrote. 'He was a sturdy child but suffered from dreadful bouts of sickness. I lived in a caravan on the moors and my husband worked nights. One night I was, as usual, on my own and had given the baby his bedtime feed. It was summer and the nights were light. Suddenly, he was sick everywhere. I was terrified, so I grabbed nappies and feed and set off down the lonely glen, walked up the steep hill and caught a bus to my mother's where I left the baby once the doctor had been. Then I made the return journey, glad to be home before dark. I was toiling up the final yards to the caravan when I heard a voice, say "Go and bring your baby back." Only lately, have I wondered why this didn't strike me as unusual at the time, but without pausing, I turned back, fetched the baby and once again made the exhausting two and a half miles uphill. It was dark by the time I got back to the caravan. Again I heard the voice telling me what to do. For three days I fed the baby only glucose and water during the day and put no clothes on him and left him in the shade. On the third night, I fell asleep as usual. Later I woke up with the knowledge there was a presence in the caravan. I quickly sat up and called out, thinking my husband had come home early because he was sick. We were far away from street lights or even the reflections from the city lights below and I always kept my curtains closed. Yet plain to see, next to the little cot beside the bed, was a small figure, about five feet four inches tall and surrounded by a soft light. It was cowled and I saw no face. I watched unafraid. When the figure and the light faded. I lay down and fell asleep again, knowing my baby would be all right. He was never sick again. I felt no motherly love for the baby until then. He had always been well cared for, but I hadn't really loved him. I now believe the experience was meant to form a bond and it made me feel much more responsible for the child.'

Judy's experience appears to have acted as a trigger for a dramatic improvement in her relationship with her child. Was it the baby's guardian angel who came to tell her to 'fetch your baby back' and appeared beside the cot or was it Judy's conscience on a dark, lonely night where exhaustion combined with looking after a sick baby could have caused hallucinations? It could be argued that the command to repeat the long journey to her mother's was Judy's unconscious way of expiating any guilt she felt for being a bad mother or it could have been a nudge from some occult force to put the mother-baby bond on the right footing. The case seems impossible to prove either way but that seems less important than the fact that mother and baby are doing well.

But a child's involvement with the supernatural need not necessarily be a bad thing. Sometimes children grow up in a world where the normal and paranormal co-exist happily and this can be an enriching, if unconventional, experience. Lilian is a charismatic character, living in a wooden chalet set in a magnificent garden, so that you can believe it is in the heart of the country. But less than a mile away is suburban sprawl and a modern shopping precinct that could be any town in Britain. I visited her to hear about her childhood, for she is a third-generation psychic brought up with two psychic grandmothers and a mother and father with the gift of second sight. Now people come to her for help and advice, a Tarot or a crystal ball reading, just as they did to her mother and grandmothers when more conventional methods of coping with the world failed.

Unlike some of the people I encountered, who were disbelieved or punished when they spoke of seeing ghosts or foretold the future, Lilian was brought up in an atmosphere that casually accepted the supernatural. The family home was fairly normal, not a cranky place full of witches' paraphernalia or a cult household where offerings were made to ancient gods or to Satan. At one stage of her childhood, Lilian was a very strong Christian and this faith coexisted quite happily at the time with her other beliefs.

One of Lilian's earliest memories is of having an invisible friend, an ancient Egyptian girl, though she can't remember her name. Lilian was about three at the time. The Egyptian girl seems to have been very close to Lilian, like a sister and Lilian apparently used to come out with all sorts of information about Ancient Egypt that she couldn't possibly have known at that age. But as Lilian grew older, her invisible friend faded. Then both Lilian's grannies moved in with her family. They both read the teacups and Lilian's house became the place for local people to go to peek into the future.

For seven years, Lilian was an only child, then her brother was born, followed three years after by her sister. 'When I was little, I used to show off at tea-leaf reading sessions and by the time I was three or four I had developed my own clientele. "Let the little one do it," they used to say. Both my grandmas were strong believers in rules for the reading of the tea cups and I was made to learn and obey these rules. Then I went to a local school for a while, but didn't like it. So I changed to another village school right opposite the church. There I began casting "love spells" of my own in the playground. I must have been about five at the time. One of the other children would say, "Do a spell," and immediately I would think one up. I always had a gift for poetry, so I found it very easy to make up a song or a chorus and get the other children in the playground to dance in and out in a chain dance. Then I would throw the spell into the middle. Sometimes the petitioner would stand in the middle as well. I think my love spells always worked because people wanted them to.' The spells gave Lilian confidence at school and made her very popular.

Later she became very much a Christian. She was told by the vicar that sometimes Satan tempted people, so you had to say 'get thee behind me Satan'. 'As I was walking to school I used to be tempted by a cheeky, little devil, complete with a little forked tail. "Do so and so," he would say. I used to have to hit him away behind me, over my shoulder. When I was with someone and the devil appeared, I used to have to slip off somewhere private and hit him back.' Lilian is still not sure whether the devil was a creature from beyond or a product of her imagination and believes that you cannot know for sure whether certain apparently psychic phenomena are manifestations from within or from another quarter, from which you are tapping the energy source.

When Lilian was nearly seven she got a shadow on her lungs and had well over a year off school. She had whooping cough and scarlet fever and was taken to see a specialist, whose only treatment was that she should be allowed to live outdoors as much as possible. 'So I ran wild. It was great, absolutely fantastic.' She was encouraged to go to the woods and sleep with the window open. 'I was left to my own devices and started to see things in a different way. I got very close to nature and began to be aware of presences in the countryside around me and I started to learn to use my will-power to bring out the essences of these presences. I found myself looking at the little people in shadowy forms. I watched them, but didn't really talk to them. I was aware even then that other people didn't have the time to see them. I used to tell mum about them, but dad didn't want to know.'

Lilian should have been learning to read and write and do arithmetic, but she thinks this lack of formal education gave her time for the other areas of her brain to come out. She spent her days sitting with one of the dogs in a blissful dream state. 'You saw an idea you were having and you produced it as no one was there but the dog. I couldn't be sure if I could manifest it for other people. I never tried.' She says she learned to be a complete anarchist and her invisible friend, the little Egyptian girl re-emerged.

Eventually she went back to school. 'I knew how to make myself popular in the playground, but I was really concerned with only one thing. I knew I couldn't read but didn't want to let on to the other children that I couldn't. I could only list a few two and three letter words. The reading class was in the afternoon after playtime, so at playtime, I went to the toilet and knelt over the toilet bowl. I prayed with every ounce of my being. First, I apologised because I wasn't in a proper place to pray, but explained that it was the only place I could be on my own. Then I asked for help and I felt, as I went into the class, that me and Jesus could do it. The children were in little circles of five or six. There was a story book and each child had to read for so long, about half a page each, then the book was passed on to the next person. I hoped and prayed to Jesus I would not be the first. I knew that if the book went round the circle first, I could do it. The person on my left was chosen to start. I put my finger on each word as it was said. I suddenly realised that some of the words were made up of little words. As each child read, I found it easier to follow and by the end of the circle I found I could read. After this I went reading mad and read nearly all the books in the local library. It was one of the most wonderful moments of my life. On some sort of psychic level, I think the ability to convince myself I could do it was all I needed. It was just a question of confidence.'

When she was 14, Lilian won a scholarship to a school of art. 'I realised that I had to be careful and not put myself in the line of ridicule, so I played down my psychic abilities. It was a real culture shock to go to art college. For a time I forgot about doing spells, seeing that other people couldn't do them. However, I did carry on making predictions. They were considered acceptable. The rest, however, was best forgotten for it didn't fit into the society in which I was mixing.

Somewhere about this time, she was introduced to the Tarot cards and took to them straight away. She had always read ordinary cards, so this was just one step on from that. 'Tarot readings were considered more permissible in college society.' At the age of seventeen, Lilian came south, determined not to let anyone know she was psychic. 'I would just be an ordinary person and not let on about my powers. But I found that complete strangers at odd times sussed I knew things and could make predictions.' She married young and by nineteen had had her first child. She gave the odd reading during this time and gradually built up a clientele.

For some of the 'normal' mothers I have written about, the birth of their children created a psychic link that they had not suspected could exist. But Lilian, for all her skills, found herself as helpless as many other first-time mothers. 'My eldest child, completely blew my brains. I was so desperate to be a perfect mum, I ignored my psyche. I used to get up every hour during the night and hold a glass in front of my daughter's face to see if she was still breathing. By the second child, I'd got my act together. If Peg was restless, I could send thoughts to calm her down. With the younger ones I could send thoughts to stop them crying to the cot or pram from wherever I was round the house.

How did Lilian's children feel about growing up with a psychic mother? Lesley, Lilian's youngest daughter, is the one who has followed most closely in her mother's psychic footsteps. She is an artist by profession, but at weekends Lesley can be found telling fortunes at fêtes and fairs, casting the runes but mainly reading the Tarots. Lilian's eldest daughter has taken a more conventional path and Peg, her second child, keeps her psychic side fairly low key. However, Peg's son, George, seems set to become a fifth generation psychic.

Lilian's children were, like her, brought up in the countryside. Lesley told me: 'It was really beautiful where we lived and we children used the countryside as our garden. It seemed very magical. We lived in an old house at a crossroads. There was the lane and a big mansion that used to be a sanatorium. The mansion was completely empty and we used to play in the garden. We used to call it the 'Japanese' or 'magic' garden. There was a 'magical' lake and we used to run inside the empty house. We had lots of bird friends and used to talk to them. When it was sunset, we used to hear the 'drummer' in the sky, beating the drums and we knew it was time to go home. We knew we had to get home before the sun set or we'd be goners. We would run down the little hill like billyo.

'We used to see figures and Peg saw ghosts. There was a house down the road that was haunted. Peg stayed in the sister's bedroom there and once she woke up to see a blue lady sitting on the bed, drinking a blue cup of tea. Another time in the same bedroom, Peg looked up and saw a man in a turban with a sword, waving it above her head. Peg was about eight at the time and I was a year younger. Then once when she was playing outside our house, Peg suddenly came dashing in. There were two pillars we used to climb on – marking the entrance where a big gate once was and four ghosts were sitting on the pillars. They were four children.'

Lesley's interest in runes began in her childhood. 'When I was young I used to throw stones and twigs and made amulets and charms with them. Everything was a ritual. I used to see the past and future with the runes I made. I made up my own meanings for the symbols I put on them. I could tell who a person's family was and could always see their parents. I would sometimes read them for friends and family, but mainly preferred to play with them by myself. I used to feel stones and know them to be magic and powerful. You have to let that ability develop naturally.'

Lesley says she could tell the future, but the family tradition was never to foretell doom, only to give warnings. 'I didn't realise I was brought up differently from other kids until I was about twenty-five. Mum was very in tune with the universal laws. She did spells at home. I didn't meet many people as a child because we lived in the country so I didn't realise mum was different. When we moved to a flat in another country place, mum lived in a shed in the garden – I was about eleven at the time. Mum would keep all these mysterious things in her shed and I can remember this woman walking past our house, looking over and crossing herself.'

From about the age of eight Lesley gave Tarot readings and often helped people with the zodiac. She was nicknamed 'Witchey-poo' at school because of the publicity following an incident in which she displayed her talent for knowing that something bad was about to happen. 'Some friends and I had just got off the school bus one morning and we were waiting at the kerb for the cars to pass so we could cross over to get to school. Two hundred yards down the road, a car turned out of a junction into the main road and moved towards us. I then turned to my friend Sylvie and for no apparent reason said, "I think that woman is going to run you over." The woman stopped the car so we could cross the road, but I then noticed she was shaking and there was something strange about her. Sylvie stepped off the kerb and for some reason I tried to stop her, but the woman started up the car and ran Sylvie over. Fortunately Sylvie was only badly shaken and bruised.'

Lesley describes her own son as very gifted and creative, with tremendous insight, but it is George, Peg's six-year-old son, who seems to be pursuing the more direct psychic line. He calls himself the Spirit Warrior and he lives only a few doors away from Lesley's house, which is where I met him. He was eager to tell me about his runes which he made himself. 'I found the stones on the floor and put marks on them.' His aunt and grand-mother told me he used to throw them to see if he was going to have a good day at school.

'At night things happen,' George told me. 'On mum-my's bed, I see little people. There is a little man and a really big one with a round football head. The little one just walks around and kicks you. They don't say anything they're just smiley. They are quite friendly. If I tell mum, they just go away. Then there are other monsters flying around the bed in different colours and there is a middle-sized knight who walks about. He comes in armour and has a shield, but no sword. He talks about different wars, about how they all started and things like that. I told the knight about my Grandad who was called George as well. He sat on a bomb in the war and it exploded.'

Will George turn his back on the psychic world as he grows up. Many men do seem to find it hard to incorporate the supernatural into their lives in the same way that women do? Or will George go on to develop his abilities and carry them through to the sixth generation?

12

Other Lives

Sometimes children seem to have existed before in another life. Lorna wrote: 'My daughter's baby was born on Christmas Eve. She was the first girl in the family. When she was six months old, she died. But I kept saying to myself, "She will come back." Two years later my daughter had another little girl, Suzy, with blue eyes just like the first. When Suzy was two years old, she accidentally found some photos of the baby's grave covered with flowers. She picked the photos up, ran to her mother and said "My flowers, mummy, mine, mine." "No," said her mother. But Suzy kept insisting they were hers. "Dark, dark trees," she said. "Me frightened. Me go way. But me come back, me not go away again." 'There was a row of tall trees near the baby's grave.'

Was Suzy the reincarnation of her dead sister? Or had she picked up conversations about her and perhaps half-understood that her parents took flowers to the grave, so that when she saw the photograph with the flowers she had become jealous and decided to claim them.

Transmigration between species is regarded as a distinct possibility by believers in reincarnation. A particularly noble creature may attain human rebirth, while a worthless individual may be demoted. David, a perfectly ordinary schoolboy, had obviously lived a very worthy past existence. He told me: 'I was playing crazy golf with a friend when an elderly lady approached me and said she had seen me before. I had never seen her in my entire life. She thought for a while and then said "Yes, I've definitely seen you somewhere before." Well, by now we were thinking that the lady was senile. Then she said that I was her pet dog who was killed by a garbage truck. Now we were really convinced she was senile. Then she said that if she was right, I should have a lump on the back of my neck. So to prove her wrong, I felt behind my neck and there was the lump there, just where she said.

The American parapsychologist, Dr Scott Rogo, who has studied reincarnation for more than 20 years, says he has known hundreds of cases where children have talked about past lives, usually before the age of four and before they could read or had been taken to the cinema. These children usually give their previous names and very often have a birthmark which relates to the previous life. It could be argued that even a small child could have had time to absorb a surprising amount of information on which to base 'another life'. But that cannot account for the apparent transmission of accident marks that both Dr Rogo and others have discovered. A case studied by Dr Ian Stevenson is that of the Pollock twins from Hexham in Northumberland. Their father believes them to be the reincarnation of their twin sisters, who were killed in an accident in 1957. The younger twin, Jennifer, has a thin white line on her brow exactly where the dead younger twin, Jacqueline, had a scar from falling off her bicycle when she was two. Jennifer also has a thumb-print birthmark on her left hip in the same place as Jacqueline had.

Older children and teenagers will sometimes recognise a place in a way that seems more than the normal 'deja vu'. Sometimes a teenager will know the way around some old house they have never been in before or say 'there's a dent half way along that table' and there it is. Is it imagination or is it almost certain that there would be a dent in the centre of an old table or is it the memory of a past life? Janet felt all through her childhood that she was trying to remember something, though she didn't know what. She would say over and over again, 'I am Janet Elizabeth but am I?' 'I was always fascinated by Victorian bric-a-brac. Once I was given a gold annual dated 1840. Though I was only a little girl, I was very excited by the fashions in it. I felt they meant something to me. But it was not till I was grown up that I suddenly said, "I am Sarah" and stopped wondering what it was I had to remember. I suddenly knew all about Sarah, a Victorian, who was born in Edinburgh but lived in London. She was quite a privileged person, but always worked hard helping people who were in need. So I started calling myself Sarah, because I realised that was my real name.'

Dr Ian Stevenson believes that a child afraid of water without reason may have drowned in a past life and that traumas in one life are frequently carried forward to the next. Sue for no apparent reason was terrified of confined spaces and especially spiral staircases. During a session with a psychic counsellor, she was put in a trance and regressed to a life which seemed to be set somewhere in the Middle Ages. She felt herself reliving a childhood in which she was shut in a dungeon at the age of about twelve and left to die. 'There were rats and it was horrible,' she told me. Although she is now an adult with a child of her own and holds a responsible job, Sue found herself so moved by the regression that she started sobbing, 'I'm all alone and I'm going to die.' Apparently the little boy, as she was in her past life, was taken down spiral stairs to the dungeon.

Her psychic counsellor treated the memory of this past life almost as a conventional psychotherapist would deal with a traumatic childhood event that has been repressed for years and suddenly resurfaced. As in conventional therapy, she made Sue relive the event, then move away from it and acknowledge that it was something that had happened in the past and that Sue could now go forward. Freud's basic tenet is that all our traumas stem back to childhood. The question that Sue's experience raises is – which one? Was she reliving a previous childhood or saying something about this one? Whatever the truth, the psychic method proved valuable to Sue who is now much less scared of confined spaces and spiral staircases.

In a psychic session I was allowed to watch I saw a regression into childhood where a woman found herself in a street market hiding from her master, a chimney sweep. 'Naa, I ain't frightened of him,' she sniffed. She said she was eight-years-old and that she had died of consumption when she was nine. Later she told me that as a nine-year-old child in this life, she was found to have a shadow on her lungs. In another session, a woman found herself to have been the lonely eight-year-old daughter of a

Victorian solicitor. As I watched, her voice did change to that of a child and she had to be coaxed to talk. But all past lives are not exotic. One woman went back to being a crippled boy who was sent out to scare crows. He died in his early twenties from cold and hunger.

Adopted children will always wonder about their real parents and will often spend a great deal of time and effort in later life looking for them. 'I want to stay with you but I want to go back and see my other family,' is the type of plea that is familiar to many adoptive parents. But coming from three-year-old James, it threw his mother completely. He is her natural child and has never lived anywhere else but their home.

'It all started gradually,' his mother Carolyn told me. 'James would talk about his other family but he was obviously anxious not to upset us. He said he had lived with another family before and he did want to be with us, but he would also like to go and see them. At first we treated it very lightheartedly and humoured him. Then he started talking about another father and mother and a sister, which was also strange because his own sister, Sarah, had not been born then. He also talked about a vehicle his "other family" used to have which appeared to be horse-drawn. There wasn't anything we could do, because we didn't know where to take him to see this family, but it was awful because at one stage he was getting very distressed about not seeing them.'

Carolyn coped as best as she could with all this, but not very successfully. 'He would constantly say, "You know, when I lived in the white house" and become more and more distressed and start to cry, begging us to take him to the white house. "All right, I'll take you," I sometimes promised, but, of course, I had no idea where it was and realised I had gone too far. There were tears on several occasions – "I want to go now, please take me," he used to insist. It was so frustrating. We didn't know where to take him. "You know, you know," he would cry. Then suddenly it stopped.'

Was this a case of reincarnation or of some sort of fantasy world which had taken root in the boy's mind at a very early age? It raises many problems. Suppose James' parents had found a white house that fitted his description and there had been a family living there who had lost a son just before James was born. What would their reaction have been if James had arrived and said, 'Hello, I used to be your child.' It might have served only to reopen the wound of grief for the bereaved parents or they might have rejected James, which would have been a severe psychological blow to the boy. Or, worst of all, the bereaved parents might have demanded the return of 'their' child. A reincarnation custody case might not have stood up in court and the effect on James of having his loyalties suddenly split between past and present parents would have been horrific.

Although James no longer mentions the family in the white house, his strong feelings of having another home appear to have surfaced in another way. He is now nine and says that he has a home on another planet, where he goes when he cannot sleep. His sister who is five insists he has taken her there and that the trees were red. 'He is an insomniac,' says Carolyn, 'and says that on his planet, the people stay awake at night and go to sleep in the day, so he is able to go there at night. He is very reluctant to talk about it because people tend to tease him, so he tends to clam up.'

Perhaps the most surprising aspect, especially in view of his talk of his former family, is that on Planet X, as James calls it, he is not a king or a galactic hero fighting monsters. He has a house and a mother and father to whom he is an only child and lives a remarkably ordinary life. 'In the garden, bananas grow on trees,' he told me. 'The leaves are yellow and the bananas are brown when they are ripe. I've got my own house in the garden. All the houses are red, like clay, except the walls are completely flat with no bumps. Usually every house has a computer in the wall. My dad just shoots stars and things and mum does the housework with computerised gadgets. I don't go to school. We go to the park. It is like the local park except that it's got a slide like a spiral that spins round. I don't play with anyone really. It's always light there. I look at the clock and come back when I think it's teatime. That gets me back at four o'clock in the morning to my other house. Then I sleep till morning.'

James told me he gets to his Planet X in a small spaceship which is operated by remote control. There is room for three people on board but usually he is the only one, although his sister Sarah told me that one night when she couldn't sleep, James took her along as well. She can't remember much except the grass was a different colour – James says it is grey – and the people were nice. But she was naughty and picked some apples, which were orange, but had stalks like ours. 'I suppose I might stop going one day,' James added. 'I don't think I'd be very sad about that.' 'What about your other family on Planet X,' I asked, 'wouldn't they mind?' 'I don't know,' he said.

Carolyn recalls that the Planet X stories started when

James was about four-and-a-half. 'His grandfather had said that James was different from the rest of us and added jokingly that he must be an alien. Soon after, James very matter-of-factly announced that his grandfather had been right and that he did come from somewhere else.' Chance remarks like the grandfather's can trigger off unexpected reactions from children. If a child does feel different from the rest of the family for whatever reason, he or she might insist that they do not belong and have come from somewhere else – a situation which can become quite upsetting for some parents. But the interesting feature of James's case is that the insistence that he came from somewhere else began so early and that he was obviously not trying to upset his parents because of some real or imagined grievance, but kept saying he wanted to stay with them.

Magic lands abound in folklore around the world. The idea seems to satisfy a basic human need and it is no wonder that children create them. The son of Jean Piaget, the psychologist, had an imaginary land which he created for his imaginary characters. But, Piaget recorded, from the age of about seven, he gradually became less interested in it. For Jessica, her 'world' was a magic place to which she escaped for many years, whenever she was unhappy. There no one could get to her to tease her about her severe dyslexia. She is now seventeen and emotionally stable, although she had many problems in her childhood. Her mother was very loving, but often ill and sometimes depressed. Although intelligent, Jessica could hardly read or write and was not diagnosed as severely dyslexic until her early teens. The special unit, at the boarding school to which she was eventually sent found her the second worst case it had ever encountered. This disability brought her a lot of teasing, so she retreated into a magical land – as a psychologist said, 'an eminently sane reaction to an unstable world'. Jessica was not rejecting the world, but reacting to the world's rejection of her. Whether psychic or psychological, her special world, Isley, enabled her to come through her bad experiences and emerge confident, creative and mature. 'It had its own alphabet,' Jessica told me, 'and I had my own way of writing the name – although this could be linked up with my dyslexia. Isley was underground – but it was somehow also in an open-air place. You got there through a special tunnel under a tree. There was a train service – I was fascinated by trains and those little bumper type cars, like you saw in the Rupert Bear stories. There was bright sunlight like in the Wizard of Oz. It was a perfect place. Everything there was designed for children, but I never saw people there. There were only good witches with black cloaks on their heads but no bodies. There were animal people, rats or mice. I could go to Isley when I liked. I would sometimes try to explain it to friends, but I could tell from their eyes they were not sure what the hell I was talking about.

'My doll, Hamble, which I have had since the day I was born, and I were rulers of Isley. We would go there whenever I was unhappy or teased at school. I knew none of my friends could get there. We would wander around for what seemed like hours, through all the streets and roads of the various towns. It was so nice. In a way it has never gone away. I still remember it all very clearly although I don't think about it much now. There's a picture of it in my mind as I am talking to you – going down into the earth and down the tunnel, the train station, being on the train and in the dark square miners' cave and then emerging into the open air and my castle. Isley became less important to me when I went to my new school with the dyslexia unit.'

For some children, the visits to the happier land are fleeting but still memorable. Marianne writes: 'When I was four-years-old, I fell asleep with my eyes open. I remember visiting a beautiful land where colours were deeper and richer and brighter, but I was still aware of my home surroundings. I was in a trance. At the time there were family problems and I was unhappy. I felt unwanted and left out, so I tapped into a power I knew I had and used it to escape.' Her mother and elder brother sympathised with her but for the rest of the family, imagination and sensitivity were out of step. Sadly, Marianne had a nervous breakdown in later life. Michael Jackson, the psychologist at the Alister Hardy Research Centre, has suggested a link between badly-handled early psychic experiences and later troubles. As mentioned earlier, he sees both as due to a particularly sensitive type of temperament. What children believe happens to them, whether or not it is testably true, is a statement about how they are trying to make sense of their situation.

Having an Isley or a Planet X or thinking that you have had an earlier life could be a stage that many children go through, although some become more deeply involved than others. Most grow out of it, but some do not and this is not necessarily a bad thing, if it can be channelled in the right direction. The late J. R. R. Tolkien's *Lord of the Rings* is a remarkable example of the imaginary world taken to extremes. He not only produced detailed maps of Middle Earth in which his Hobbits had their remarkable adventures, but also produced an elfin language with its own runic alphabet, songs and folklore. Had he not been the highly respected Merton Professor of English Language and Literature at Oxford, such an obsessive concern with fantasy might have marked him down as a suitable case for treatment. As it was, he turned his private world into an international best-seller.

But where does a fantasy land end and magic one begin? I am not sure there is any division. Because the child enters the land, it becomes real for him or her. Can we be absolutely certain there is no Planet X, just because we lack the personal magic to get there?

13

Beyond the Body

The trouble with children is often that they do not know their limitations. In an episode from the *Daily Mirror's* Perishers cartoon strip, Baby Grumpling is considering life and says to himself, 'If people can go forwards and backwards and sideways why can't they go up?' And seeing no good reason why they shouldn't, he starts to levitate. Then his sister, Maisie, arrives on the scene and tells him, 'Grumpling, if you want to live with people, you've got to learn to obey the rules.'

Many children have broken bones to show for their early attempts at flying before they learned the rules. But some can remember breaking those rules and getting away with it. Mary recalled: 'It happened quite spon taneously when I was about three. I seemed to come out of my body and take off from the top of the stairs. I floated down, alighting gently at the bottom.' Cicely also told me: 'I was floating outside myself and came to the top of the staircase outside my bedroom door and took off, glid-

ing gently down the stairs, head first I think. It was day-
light, a summer evening. I think I was five-years-old. In
those days one was sent to bed at set times, regardless of
the light. The next night, I went to the head of the stairs
and waited to take off, but it didn't work. I was extremely
disappointed. Flying through the air was a wonderful
sensation. If this was a dream, it was certainly no ordinary one.'

William, aged five, told his mother, Wendy, that not so
long ago he woke one night, left his body behind on the
bed and floated downstairs touching the handrail. In the
morning, he reported pinging back into his body just
before waking. He sensed the bed bouncing slightly.

Many children experience this floating down the stairs
sensation. Though some of the heavier psychoanalysts
can put 'deep' interpretations on floating and flying, from
a psychological point of view, it can perhaps be regarded
simply as children testing the limits of their powers,
which, of course, they may greatly overestimate. Lev-
itation has never been proven in a laboratory, but there
have been tests which have provided some evidence – not
accepted by the majority of scientists – for the existence
of 'out-of-the-body experiences', known as 'OOBEs'. In
these, the subject seems to leave his or her physical body
behind and move around in a psychic body complete with
arms and legs. I have heard of a number of cases in which
OOBEs happened quite spontaneously to children.

Lesley had her first out-of-the-body experience when
she was only seven. She told me: 'It was a sunny day and I
was sitting with my back against a tree. Suddenly I felt I
was up in the tree, sitting there. I knew I was there. It was
a copper beech tree and I could see myself sitting on the

ground in the distance down below. There were lots of people around because there was a party at our house and I was very happy, hiding from people up there. Eventually, I came down from the tree and went back into my body.'

Lesley enjoyed her experience and it served as a means of escape from all the people whom she didn't want to mix with. Whether it was imagination or an actual astral projection (as an out-of-the-body experience is sometimes termed), the experience served the same purpose. 'It made me feel good,' she said. Lesley says she has had three OOBEs, one as a child, one as a teenager and one when she was twenty. Each time she thinks it was a specific sound that seemed to trigger off the experience. 'When I was very young, the first time, it was the sound of wheels. I think it was a pram going past,' she said.

Experiments to test out-of-the-body experiences are notoriously difficult to carry out. Dr Robert Morris, now head of the parapsychology department at Edinburgh University, carried out a series of experiments on them at Duke University in America in 1973 with Dr Keith Harary, then a 20-year-old student who had already had many out-of-the-body experiences. Dr Harary attempted to leave his body to visit his pet kittens, Spirit and Soul. Spirit, who was being observed in another room by Dr Morris and his assistants during the attempts, was seen to be quieter when Dr Harary's psychic body was supposed to be soothing it. Was this coincidence or even, as some psychic investigators believe, a telepathic communication between Dr Harary and the cat? Dr Susan Blackmore, a parapsychologist, began investigating OOBEs after she apparently had one herself while at university. She now distrusts her memory of the experience, which occurred while she was under the influence of drugs, and says an actual psychic form has never been detected in a laboratory even with the most elaborate conditions and equipment. As always, the real problem remains of how what was discovered or not discovered in the laboratory bears any relation to children apparently whizzing their astral bodies up trees to avoid boring social situations.

An OOBE can be terrifying if it occurs at night and the child feels totally out of control. Wanda writes: 'I was five or six and we lived in a house with only one bedroom, so I slept with my parents. I was feeling very ill and tired. Then I remember this floating feeling and felt I was drifting up to the window. I was actually standing next to it, on a kind of box with a rail of some sort. I remember looking down on myself and my parents. We were all asleep. I started to panic and shouted, "I want to go back." I kept saying that and calling my mother and crying at the same time. I couldn't understand why nobody heard me. Suddenly I felt a drifting feeling and I was back in bed, but I didn't go to sleep. I kept looking up to the wardrobe and expected to float up there at any minute. I remember feeling so afraid. The experience was like there were two of me.' It was a long time before Wanda would sleep alone after that, even when the family moved and she had her own bedroom.

Norma is in her seventies, but can still remember her frightening OOBE at the age of eleven. 'I went to bed as usual. I was not ill or anything, but that night I thought I woke up, but I had left my body and was looking down on myself sleeping from somewhere near the ceiling. It was

an old house with high ceilings. From the ceiling pro-
truded a hand, a right hand, a man's because there was
part of a shirt cuff. I took hold of the hand and it began to
draw me upwards and a voice I did not recognise as male
or female said, "Come with me." I said, "No, I can't
come. My work here is not done," and let go of the hand.
The next moment I was in my body again, gasping for
breath and desperate to get enough air in my lungs. For a
few seconds, I really thought I would die, but gradually I
recovered. All this is as vivid today as when it happened.'

Sylvia too believed for a moment that she was going to
die. 'It happened when I was eleven. I was lying in my bed
and trying to get to sleep. Then I could see my own body
lying on the bed and my sister, who was in the bed next to
mine. I didn't float to the ceiling but stayed suspended
between the beds. But the strange thing was that I felt as
if I was a mass of black dots. Next thing I knew I was back
in my body. The next day, I told my mother I had thought
I was dying and she gave me some brandy to calm me
down.'

Were Norma's and Sylvia's experiences bad dreams or
did the children really leave their bodies? Many OOBEs
happen at night or first thing in the morning. Is this
because the conscious mind is at its least active then,
thus removing constraints on psychic activity or is the
imagination simply more active when the body is not?
Psychologists can argue that OOBEs result from unfulfilled wishes, projected on to a second life that the subject can control – a sort of super-self! This would be especially attractive to children. For quite young children, an
out-of-the-body type trance can be a way of escaping
from a reality in which he or she may feel rejected.

Karl's need to feel powerful and superior to his companions, with whom he was less able to compete in physical terms, is implicated in his account of his out-of-the-body experience. 'I withdrew from the melée (of a football game with friends) and walked to the school gates. I started to feel sleepy – as if I was dropping into a trance. A soft breeze was blowing against my face. The evening was soft and warm. The warmth consumed my body as if the sun was shining directly onto my flesh. The warmth was more and more intense. I attempted to wake myself from this dream-like state, but found I could not. The same feeling took control of my body and thoughts. Suddenly I found myself above, way above, the others and my own physical body, calmly observing my friends. As I remained there, floating thirty feet above the ground, I was in no way aware of being attached to a physical body or physical existence. It was as if part of my mind had decided to take its leave. I sensed a strange kind of dominance over my earthbound companions. I am up here. You are down there. At this, I felt even more satisfied, complete, above human understanding and knowledge. Suddenly one of my friends shouted my name. The voice that replied so angrily "Shut up" seemed very distant, yet I am certain it was my voice. My friend called out a second time and suddenly, I leapt back into my body. Then I remained rooted to the spot, dazed and confused.

Flo's OOBE stopped her from getting the attention she so desperately wanted. 'I am 65,' she wrote. 'When I was 12, I was very ill in bed for weeks. We couldn't really afford a doctor (in those days you had to pay for a visit) but I was so ill that for the first time in my life mum said the doctor could come to see me. I heard the doctor come upstairs and pause on the landing. The door opened and in he came, but he didn't talk to me at all. He was looking at somebody in the bed and I was up on the ceiling above the mantelpiece. I spoke to him but he ignored me. I was angry and thought "Well who's he looking at down there," and at that split second I found that I had moved across the room with no conscious effort and was looking up over the doctor's shoulder. To my amazement I realised I was back in bed. I do not remember any more, but I seemed to know instinctively not to tell anyone or they would laugh.

Youngsters who experiment with OOBEs can sometimes go a bit too far. Alan explains: 'When I was ten, I was given permission to stay up late to listen to the radio. The time was about 9.30 pm. I remember clearly thinking it must be possible for your spirit or soul to detach itself from the physical body and roam free. I sat still. I don't know for how long but I suddenly realised all was still and silent and that I felt truly free. I wasn't frightened. I was outside my body and looking down at myself. In fact I was studying myself hard when suddenly I was conscious of movement on my left-hand side and the door opened. My sister Eleanor walked in. She looked at my physical body and screamed. Without any effort on my part, I found myself whole again. Then I asked my sister if she was all right. She was very upset and told me she thought I was dead. She said I was totally empty like a shell. I was going to tell her what had happened, but she became pretty angry and accused me of trying to frighten her. She threatened to tell my parents but I reached a pact with her.'

Gordon frightened himself with an out-of-the-body experience when he was twelve. For a year had been experimenting with his dreams, trying to control them. 'My mother used to call me every morning in time for breakfast. One trick I played on her was to rattle my shoes under my bed and shout, "I'm coming." This particular morning, I must have dropped back into a doze. My mother lost her temper. She came upstairs and gave a sharp knock on my door. "Gordon, get out of bed," she cried. Immediately, I found myself suspended about one foot above my body and bed. I clearly saw my body on the bed below. The situation was very real, indeed more real than most of life's experiences. "God, I'm dead," I thought. I embraced my body below on the bed, thinking, "I've got to get back." I hugged the body with my arms. Then I remember looking up at the ceiling with relief – I was back in my body again. At the same time, I could feel my heart pounding fast and I remember my mother entering the room and remarking, "What on earth's wrong with you?" "Oh, I'll be all right in a minute or two," I said. "Go away. I'll be down soon." With hindsight, the remarkable thing was she did just that. The result of my experience was an overwhelming sense of security. Life doesn't just stop here on earth. The only problem has been getting anyone to believe me.'

Psychic forms may never have been detected under laboratory conditions, but according to the accounts I came across close relatives sometimes perceive them. When Connie was a child, she was very ill in hospital with meningitis. 'After my parents had visited me, they went home and went to bed. In the middle of the night, my mother woke up and said to my father that she felt I was in bed with them. Then my father also felt my presence.

The following evening when they visited me, I told them that I thought I had slept with them that night. From that day I started to recover.' Though Connie's parents did not actually see her, they did feel her presence. Had both parents and child tuned in at a time of distress when each would be thinking of the other? Bedtime when a child is absent is particularly poignant and Connie was probably thinking of home and family? Or did Connie 'travel' home for comfort? The experience or her belief in it may have triggered some psychological strength that gave her immune system a kick.

Pauline often visited her father, Phil, who had separated from her mother, and got on very well with his new partner, Mandy. He had tried to reassure the little girl that although he didn't live with her all the time, he would always be there if she needed him. Kids are notorious for taking parents at their word, often with bizarre results. One evening, Phil and Mandy were sitting watching television, when Phil felt a chill run through him and all the hairs on the back of his neck standing on end. He couldn't understand what was happening, but men can be very unobservant. It was Mandy who eventually said, 'Can't you see her sitting over there – it's Pauline?' His little girl had apparently 'popped back' in her astral body to test her father's words!

OOBEs seem to be related to a phenomenon described as the 'near death experience' or NDE, often reported by people who have come close to death through illness or an accident. They seem to leave their bodies and glimpse some sort of afterlife. Dr David Lorimer, director of the International Association for Near Death Studies, has received many accounts from adults and teenagers relating childhood as well as more recent NDEs. Children's reports of NDEs differ from those of adults in that, although they are less elaborate they have a special pictorial quality.

Phoebe had a very bad attack of scarlet fever as a child before the Second World War. She was not expected to last the night in the old fever hospital, where she was cared for by nuns. Later in life, she told her daughter that she remembered looking down on her body that was lying on the bed and seeing the nuns and the doctor standing next to it. She remembers feeling very much at peace and floating down a spiral. She could hear soothing music, but it was not being played on any specific instrument. She was going down the spiral into something clean, white and cotton-woolly, when suddenly she felt something cold pressed on her forehead and was back on the bed. A nun had put a cold sponge on her head. Without this intervention, Phoebe would have gone on down the spiral, where she saw a shadow beckoning her. It did not have a face, but was a nice shape.

The simplest stories involve the child floating above his or her body. Mike was nearly five. 'It was Christmas. I remember it as if it was yesterday. I was very excited that Christmas was almost upon us in spite of the war. I remember rushing out to the corner shop to buy my dad cigarettes in the freezing weather without a coat before my mother could stop me (shopkeepers served anyone in those days). Anyway the next thing I recall, was being extremely ill, so much so that my mother set up a bed for me in the front room next to the fire. After that I don't remember much except for one vivid memory. Suddenly I was floating above the bed. Everything, including my mind, was crystal clear. I could see myself lying on the bed, blond-haired and angel-faced, with my eyes closed. I remember being fascinated at the sight of my nostrils pumping in and out as I laboured to breathe and I remember thinking, "Wow, I do look sick." Being so young, I assumed that everybody could get outside their bodies and see themselves. This was my last thought before I was aware of a cold stethoscope being pressed to my chest and saw my old family doctor looking at me and saying to my mother, "You almost lost him. He's got pneumonia and only pulled through with your care."'

Oona also had very bad pneumonia when she was about seven. 'I can recall being in bed in my parents' bedroom with a fire in the grate. I was very hot, in pain and distressed. The next second I was high above the bed, looking down and all the pain was gone. I was floating and looked down at myself and my parents and felt a bit sad for them, but happy for myself that I could leave my body behind. As I turned to the top corner of the room, out of the golden haze, my mother's voice said, "Oona, oh, Oona," and the next minute I was back in my bed with all the pain. Afterwards I looked back on the experience with some surprise, but dared not relate it to anyone for fear of ridicule. But it was so real to me and still is, that I have never feared death since. If this life was all we had, then it would be illogical and rather a poor deal for some.'

It has been pointed out that children will often claim to have seen living rather than dead relatives during an NDE. Rob saw his mother trying to pull him back. He was nine and a first appendix operation had left part of the organ still inside him and it had burst. 'By the time of my second operation, my condition was serious and at one point clinical death occurred. I can only recall two images. The first was of looking down on my own body lying on the operating table and being turned over by green-clad surgeons and nurses. This image was particularly vivid and despite its goriness was not associated with any pain or distress. The second image was of a blackness with a pinpoint of light far off in the distance. I felt drawn to the light, but there was a feeling that I didn't really want to move towards it. My mother was with me in this scene, trying to pull me back from the light. There was also a wind rushing past us towards the light. Again this image was startlingly clear, unlike many other things I remember from that time. I remember little else except coming round after the operation in total panic, made worse by the fact that I couldn't move properly due to the after-effects of the operation.'

Rob does not see this experience as a spiritual one. 'As an atheist. I cannot accept any talk of the soul. Rather I view it as a function of the chemical changes that occur in your brain on death.' However, for some people, a childhood NDE is not only more real than reality, it colours their whole attitude to life. They may feel that they should have died and, in some extreme cases, later attempt suicide. Jessie who had her NDE while suffering from peritonitis says, 'I seemed to float outside my body and along an empty corridor towards and then into a brilliant light with indefinable shades of pastel-like colours. There were what I can only describe as billions of beautiful shimmering forms, only outlines as they were all cloaked in whitish-like garments of transluscent light. I longed to be able to tell my parents not to grieve and if only they knew how joyously happy I was, they would rejoice instead. Then suddenly I was back in my body again. I often wish I had not been brought back and then I would not have had to live through the many problems that have beset my life and I would have died in total peace. Death can come at any time and I have no fear of it.'

Josephine is now twenty-two but her life since her NDE, during an operation in France as a child of twelve, has been spent trying to recreate her experience. 'Everything went too fast for me,' she recalls. 'One minute I was in a deep dark sleep and then suddenly I was in a place with mid-pinkish clouds everywhere, hazy and soft with a pinkish light. It was very comforting. Next I was wandering through rooms and there was beautiful music. It was so smooth, soft and harmonious. I was so much at ease and felt so relieved and peaceful. I floated through these rooms at a higher level than I walked at that age. In fact it seemed, I nearly grazed the ceiling. It seemed to me we were looking for something. Some quiet presence was with me. Then we were in a room and there below me the doctors, masked and gowned, bent over what I saw was my body. "More glucose," one was saying. Then I had a shock. It seemed like they were talking right next to me, yet I was looking at them from above. "Which do you wish?" insisted the presence. "You don't have to go back. The choice is up to you." There was no pressure to choose, but I thought about mum and dad and in a flash I felt I was back lying in the operating theatre. There was no whoosh or warning that I was about to return. It was a great shock that it happened at the moment I thought about my loved ones. The experience made me feel very strange. After I came round, I spoke to no one about it, but I remembered how happy I had been in that state and this made me either very enthusiastic or extremely unhappy about things. I once worked at a fun fair when we lived in the United States, taking rides in a desperate attempt to create the feeling of flying. I cut my hair and had it dyed red and took delight in anything pink and puffy. While I lived with my parents, I could control my desire to return, but the moment I came back to England to university, it was all set free. Sometimes I seemed to be controlled by something that was not me and I wondered if I had brought something back with me from the other side. I have often regretted the choice I made to return, though there are times when I am proud of that choice.'

While some NDEs leave a scar, others are quite magical and with young children religion and magic can be mixed together. The vividness and strange imagery of six-year-old Jacques' NDE were not part of a child's normal visions of angels or God. 'I had had a fall from a considerable height, landing head first on concrete and when I arrived at the hospital the doctors pronounced me dead and issued a death certificate. I was placed in a room that was constructed of marble and left there three days. On the third day, a nurse came in, saw a slight movement and found that I was alive. All I can recall during that time is floating along a rough-hewn tunnel with walls that looked as if they were made of copper and gold lit by firebrands. I felt no fear and continued down the tunnel till I came to a round chamber cut in this strange copper and gold rock and there, seated on a beautifully designed marble throne was this enormous figure of a man in a white robe, with long, flowing white hair and a beard. He looked as old as time itself and yet as young as a boy. I ran

towards this force of love, strength, power, light and perfection and suddenly, a look of foreboding came over his
face. He raised his hand and I could go no further. Then
with a lovely smile, that hand gently pushed me back with
the words "Not now, not now" echoing in my ears. I shall
always believe it was then that I came back from the
dead.' This experience, described in later life was probably made more elaborate by adult experience and reflection. But the story itself has the vividness and pictorial qualities of a child's perceptions.

The act of giving birth can sometimes hurl the mother
into something similar to an NDE even when her life is
not in danger. For want of a better term I have coined the
phrase, 'near birth experience' or NBE. It is included in
this book on the psychic world of children because it
appears to be triggered off by the baby. Psychically or
psychologically, the mother seems to be able to glimpse
into another world as her baby enters this one and though
she may be in no danger of dying during the experience,
she may believe she has died. Birth is a moment when a
woman's link with the material, logical world is at its
weakest. Whether you believe that a child comes to this
world from another more spiritual dimension, 'trailing
clouds of glory' as Wordsworth put it, or whether you
view birth simply as a child's passage from the intraute-
rine world to the mother's arms, the baby's moment of
entry is one of intense physical, emotional, psychological
and perhaps psychic energy. As with near death experiences, near birth experiences may be wonderful and
give a woman a new insight into life. Or they may be absolutely terrifying. But this is not surprising since birth
itself can be the greatest or most painful and humiliating

moment of a woman's life.

Jane recalled that before she gave birth, she passed out. 'I started to move really fast from the bottom of a tunnel to where, nearly at the top, a lady was waiting. She was pretty and there was a very bright light which seemed to glow from her body. Then the lady put her hands on her ears and screamed, "Nooo!" like an echo and I went back down the tunnel as fast as I came up. When I got back into my body and woke up, I said, "I've just died." My husband replied, "You just passed out." "No," I said, "I've just died." He laughed and wouldn't believe me. I remember wanting to go back up the tunnel even though I didn't quite reach the top. Women understood when I told them about my experience, but I don't think many men can accept such reality.'

When people have experienced NDEs during operations, drugs and a lack of oxygen have been suggested as possible causes. But Jane underwent her near birth experience without drugs, although she did pass out. Liz Cornish, a rebirthing expert, commented: 'All our lives are about death and rebirth and it is possible to touch on a higher level of consciousness, linked in this instance with the birth. When women give birth they can sometimes relive their own birth experiences and can indeed heal their own birth traumas. There could be a release of intense psychic energy at such times.'

Near birth experiences often seem to occur when the birth is difficult or there is intense pain. Sue recalls: 'I was in labour with my first child and I was in great pain. Suddenly everything went very dark. I heard a loud banging noise, as if made by a large hammer. There was a bright light in the distance and I seemed to be travelling towards it. It became larger and brighter. I knew with great certainty that I was going to die, but I felt so happy.' After her experience, Sue felt she was kinder and more considerate, though she thinks this might have simply been because she had matured. Her second child was born naturally (the first was a forceps delivery) and the birth, she said, was wonderful but just not the same.

For Bess, the experience began after the baby was born, when her life was not in danger and she was not under the influence of any analgesics. 'It happened the night after my first child was born, when I was only twenty. I had only recently married and my parents were abroad. I found myself feeling very lonely and frightened during labour, which was excruciatingly painful. I remember praying to God for the pain to end and to die. I had a daughter and was placed in a three-bedded room of which I was the only occupant. I dropped off into an uneasy sleep and awoke to find my nose one or two inches from the ceiling. I looked down and saw myself in the bed. I though I was looking at my twin sister. Then I realised it was me. I felt frightened momentarily, but then felt myself drifting peacefully and naturally down a dark tunnel with a bright light at the end. This seemed to happen very quickly. I arrived at the end and a person on the other side, who I could hear but not see as the light was so bright, spoke to me. The person knew who I was and seemed kind and loving. He said, "Who would look after the baby if you died?" We went through the possibilities and finally I agreed that I would have to bring my daughter up. With that I was back in my body.'

Caroline Flint, Consultant Midwife at a London hospital, told me that she had come across the phenomenon. 'I think it is the only and nearest time that a human in life comes close to experiencing death. Birth and death are flip sides of the same coin. Birth is a momentous experience and it is so overwhelming that a woman often loses control over the functioning of her body. It is a bigger experience that a woman's wedding or taking exams. Even when no analgesics are given, a woman will be in a trance-like state. If you leave a woman alone in labour, she will often "go off somewhere else" almost. Birth is so much more than a physical experience. It is a spiritual, emotional and psychic event. Some women get hallucinations after being given pethidine and gas and air, but even so, women who have not had these forms of pain relief frequently have intense birth experiences.'

The intensity of the near birth experience can have an important effect on the bonding process. Jennifer, who almost died during childbirth, is convinced that her baby shared her experience. 'I was nine months pregnant and started to bleed heavily. The doctor put an oxygen mask over my face. Next I was in a dark, dark, tunnel, which branched in two. I was travelling down this tunnel to the junction. Then I had to choose which road to take. One was jagged and bumpy and very dark. The other was smooth as silk, a pure cylinder with white light at the end. Every ounce of power that was in me pulled me towards the easy route. I screamed inside at the thought of the jagged one. Suddenly an unbelievable surge of strength, which can only be described as a dam breaking, forced me down the terrible, endless, dark, jagged tunnel, down and down. There was no escape. A voice echoed over and over in my head, "Who cares anyway, who cares anyway, who cares . . ." Then I floated up to the ceiling and saw the nurse below telling me I had a baby boy. I could see the clock on the wall. I watched myself smile, but it was not me. Then I floated down. When I woke up the doctor told me I was lucky to be alive. He called my son a miracle baby – he had nearly died too.

'Sadly I have never felt any bond with my baby. I think I could have killed him in hospital. We don't get on well even now. My husband told me that when he was born, he screamed and screamed, like he had never heard a baby cry before. I feel certain the baby had a similar experience to me and that he too would have gone down the smooth artery, if that force hadn't pulled us both the other way. I couldn't breastfeed him. I tried for a month and we both hated it. My husband is very close to him and was the first to hold him. I suppose really I will never know if my baby had the same experience as I did.'

But for Paula, her near birth experience, which occurred a short time after the birth, actually awakened her bond with her baby. 'My experience happened two days after the birth of my son. It wasn't a pleasant labour and for some reason when he was born I couldn't take to him. I was shocked because when my daughter was born, I had an overwhelming love for her, yet I didn't for my son. It was all I could do to feed him. I don't really think I liked him and I was ashamed of myself. Then two days after he was born, I was in bed and didn't feel well, though it was nothing serious. I was in the ward with two other ladies. We had settled down for the night. Next thing I floated up to the ceiling. It was very dark and I felt very alone. I turned my head to look down and I could see myself clearly as I lay face upwards on the bed. I just kept on floating at no particular speed. I had the feeling that I may have died, but I don't think I really believed it. I remember calling out that I loved my son and wanted to go back and look after him and kiss him. I also wanted to go back for my daughter. I had to go back because I didn't want my children to have no mother. I kept saying this. I also called for the woman in the next bed to help me. The next thing I remember was being back in my body and the nurse coming in and switching on the light and saying she'd heard someone calling for help. After that I was able to bond with my son.'

To understand a child's early psychic experiences, we usually have to listen to the mother. However, this is not to say that a child is never consciously aware of such experiences. Very occasionally, it seems as if some memory is trapped and does not suffer the usual filters. Florence believes that, unlikely as it may seem, she remembers going through a near death experience when she was born. 'I was born in 1947 with no doctor or midwife in attendance. I know the majority of people would say it's impossible for a new-born baby to remember anything, but when I was born, I remember the feeling of floating up to the ceiling, then looking down on my body. I can't remember details like the wallpaper or anything, but I remember looking down and seeing my mother in bed holding me. Then I found myself in a dark place, climbing frantically up these walls. I had to get back. However, these horrific, horrible, decrepit dead people were moaning and trying to grab me with their arms. Suddenly I was going at great speed down a dark tunnel, heading towards a light – the horrible decrepit dead people had vanished. Just as I reached it, for some reason, I came away from it and that's all I remember. I was told in later years that when I was born I didn't breathe immediately and they thought I was dead, but when the doctor came he managed to revive me.'

Sir Alec Turnbull, Professor of the Nuffield Department of Obstetrics and Gynaecology at the John Radcliffe hospital, Oxford, said: 'It is not surprising some women hallucinate in childbirth. Delivering a baby without drugs, even when everything is perfectly normal, is as much as anyone can take on.' Perhaps this pressure, combined with the baby's psychic energy, allows the mother to look for a few seconds through the child's eyes into eternity.

14

Facing the Final Mystery

Nicholas was only seven when he was admitted to the ward where Jane was nursing. He was suffering from cystic fibrosis and his long-term prospects were not good at that time, 14 years ago. Jane said: 'He was very poorly and not responding to drugs and treatment. He deteriorated during the later part of the night and it looked as if he wouldn't turn the corner. He was being cared for mainly by his parents and the nurses were in and out of the single room he had been given, checking everything was all right but trying not to be intrusive. He was being cuddled on his mother's lap, when he opened his eyes and said: "Mummy, I can see the angels." Soon afterwards he died.'

Another little boy, who died at home, sat up exclaiming, 'Beautiful light, beautiful light,' just before he died and one girl was described by her mother as having a look of 'pure wonderment' at the moment of death. Physiological theories have been advanced about what happens in our bodies and brains to cause such deathbed visions. But it is perhaps a fallacy that a physiological explanation must be 'the correct one' and, of course, no one has reliably been able to quantify death itself. Tessa Williamson, a bereavement counsellor at the Helen House Hospice for terminally ill children in Oxford, has noticed that dying children do seem to mature very suddenly and it may be that at the moment of death they are able to share with their parents and nurses the glimpse they catch of another world.

For a child, when a parent dies, the world is turned upside down. The child feels angry and betrayed that the parent has left him. Prue remembers losing her father when she was still young. 'One day, soon after his death, I was feeling so utterly weary and wondered if it really was worth living, battling on without support and guidance. For a fleeting moment I was tempted to think about ending it all and momentary though this was, I suddenly saw my father standing by the window. He was deeply concerned about me and I heard him say, "You cannot reach me that way." Then he was gone, but the feeling that he was still deeply concerned about me persisted. The realisation that he was still caring about me and my future life grew stronger and I plodded on. Gradually over the years, I gave up all thoughts of trying to hasten my own end and never had any more doubts about life after death.'

Janet Boucher, the child psychiatrist, says that when a child sees a ghost, he is in a sense saying that the person he saw has not died. She feels that initially, seeing the ghost need not be harmful and can in fact do good but that what is worrying from the psychiatric point of view, is that by keeping the ghost the child will never resolve his or her grief. However, in Prue's case, seeing her father's ghost helped her to overcome her despair and suicidal tendencies and what she kept was the feeling that he did still care about her life.

Even a young child will try to make sense of death, whether of a beloved relative or even of a much loved pet. The child needs to explain what has happened to himself in his own terms. Alice came from a farming family. When she was eleven she was sent to boarding school and missed her mother desperately, as they had been very close. 'When I was twelve, I went home and found her terribly thin and frail. I implored her to see a doctor, but she refused to go while I was home. She cried when I left for school again, which was unusual and three days later she died. Her body lay in the guest room at home and when no one was around, I crept in to look at her. I drew back the sheet and instead of looking at peace, she looked as if she had screamed at the end and her lips were curled back over her teeth. She had been in pain to the last and I have never forgotten that. I couldn't cry and after that I couldn't eat or sleep properly.

'I dreamt one night I stood outside a door. I was very upset and hammered on the door. It opened slightly and I jammed my foot in to keep it open. I saw my mother in a room full of light. She seemed to be greeting old friends. Suddenly, she turned, put a finger up and came towards me. She said: "I'm happy here. Please go away. You cannot come here yet." The door closed. Soon after that dream, I started to feel better again, for I believed my mother was happy at last.'

When a child is away from home when a parent dies the shock can be immense. Ruth's premonition that she would not see her mother again perhaps prepared her for the shock. 'My mother had been ill on and off for years throughout my childhood. While my sister was waiting to take my brother and myself to the station to catch the train back to school after the holidays, I went to my mother's bedroom to say goodbye and gave her a hug and a kiss. Then as I turned towards the door, I just knew I wouldn't see her again. I went back and hugged her again. It was only my sister calling me to hurry up that made me leave and I remember having to run to catch up with her and pleading with her to look after mummy.

'On the day we heard my mother had died, neither my brother nor myself had received a letter from home. This was most unusual because in those days the post really did arrive on time and we always had letters on Monday mornings. By lunchtime I was getting quite agitated and suggested to my brother that after lessons we should go for a walk together. This was unusual in that boys and girls had different walk days and I was down to play hockey that afternoon. But I calmly disregarded all the rules and much to my amazement my brother agreed to go out. This was amazing as he usually avoided walking anywhere if he could. We spent the afternoon together and when I was returning to the girls' wing, I met my PE teacher who assured me that it hadn't mattered at all my not turning up for hockey. Then I was informed that the headmistress wanted to see me. I knew instantly what it was about. She, of course, had to tell me that my mother had died that morning. I am sure the events of that day were preparing us. There was no explanation for our letters not arriving. They had been posted as usual.'

Elisabeth Kübler-Ross, one of the pioneers of a new

approach to dying, says that children will not be horrified by the death of a brother or sister, even in the last stages of a terminal illness, if they have been involved throughout, as they then come to see their sick sibling with different eyes. But for a sibling just to 'disappear' and for the parents to be distraught with grief for the lost child, can be utterly confusing for the children left behind. When he was seven, the author J M Barrie lost his elder brother, David, in a skating accident. From being the carefree youngest brother, the next day he found himself faced by the impossible task of trying to take the place of his mother's favourite child. He became driven by the desire to imitate David so well, that his beloved mother would not notice the difference. Wearing his dead brother's clothes, he burst into his mother's room and began whistling in the special way that David used to do. It was not until many years later that he realised how deeply he must have hurt his mother.

I discussed this case with Tessa Williamson, the bereavement counsellor, who said it is devastating for the child left alive to feel that the parent wants the dead child and not him and that when this message seems loud and clear, the child will often try to be as much like their dead sibling as possible in order to feel wanted. Of course, a child may be misinterpreting a parent's grief, as was the case with Barrie, who never got over having caused his mother so much pain.

Janet Boucher feels that the glorification of a dead child can be permanently damaging to the esteem of surviving children. One teenager she knew, whose twin had died in childhood was still haunted by the feeling that the wrong twin had died. As she points out, the worst aspect is that children tend to believe that only old people die. So when a young person dies, it threatens the whole fabric of their world. They fear that they too may die. For Joanna, her sister, who died at the age of six, remains blonde, angelic and a good child, although Joanna realises that she must have been naughty sometimes. 'People used to say she was too good for this life,' said Joanna, 'and I remember as a child thinking that if I died, they'd think I was perfect. I was desperately unhappy.' Now middle-aged, she has always felt she had to live up to the memory of her dead sister.

The death of a grandparent, though obviously sad for children who may lose someone very special in their lives, is more in the natural order of things. When Geraldine's grandfather died, she was able to share the time leading up to his death. This helped her to cope, even as a child, with not only the loss of a beloved grandparent, but with the questions thrown up by death. 'I loved my grandfather dearly. When I was a child, he used to play his concertina for me and sang me many little songs. Then he became very ill. He had cancer and my mother nursed him at our house. One night I was sitting at his bedside and he looked up and smiled at someone I couldn't see. He said, "You've come for me," and the room was filled with an unearthly kind of love and peace and my grandfather looked so calm and happy, as though he was no longer in pain. The next morning he was dead. I looked at his dead body and knew I wasn't looking at my grandfather. His soul was my real grandfather. This was the beginning of my spiritual life.'

Death is a subject that concerns children from quite an early age, at first largely in practical terms. One woman told me that her young daughter had worked it out that it was okay if mummy and daddy died because the builder would look after her. At about the age of eight or nine, children can hit quite a maudlin stage as they try out ideas of dying. Greta told me, 'When I was about eight, I seemed to be making very heavy weather of life. My devoted parents and brother insisted that I had to be good to be loved, but I was a bit questioning and maverick. I decided that this earth was not for me and that I'd rather go to heaven, which for me meant Jesus. I felt sure he would understand me. Then an aunt died and it said on the tombstone "Fallen asleep", so I reasoned that if you fell asleep lying on your back with your hands crossed on your breast that was all there was to it. So one night, with a few tears for what my family would find in the morning, I managed very slowly to sink to sleep in the right position and straight into a dream about heaven. There was a large green field and I saw Jesus standing there dressed in blue and white. I ran to him, but his face was not welcoming or kind. He turned me around saying, "Not yet, Greta, not yet." I woke up feeling very stiff in the morning and wept and wept, because there I was back on earth again.'

Lucienne was eight-years-old and living in Montreal when she dreamed of death. 'I was flying higher and higher towards the sky, flying so high I shall never forget that dream. Suddenly I thought, "How shall I return to earth?" but I was not afraid. Then I arrived in a big dark tunnel. I could see a bright light, far off in the distance. I wanted to get to the light, but I couldn't get more than a short distance down the tunnel. After that I woke up and told my family that I wondered if it could be something like that when you died. It all seemed so real.'

Do children use the images we give them of Jesus and going up to heaven to weave a concrete explanation of what death is like or are they tapping into what Jung would call the 'collective unconscious', the universal symbols of all times and cultures that underlie human existence? Or did Greta and Lucienne experience a glimpse of the world beyond?

For those left behind when a child dies there is the problem of trying to cope with the unbearable. Are the ghosts of children a sign of some sort of life after death or is the loss of a child so unacceptable that the mind has to recreate the child? To write merely of paranormal incidents concerning children and death seemed to be dodging the issue, so I went to Helen House Hospice for terminally ill children to talk to Tessa Williamson and to see how bereaved families coped. 'Many parents do report the sense of a presence after a child's death – of being aware that the child is with them, although they don't actually see him. The just feel that he is around,' said Tessa. 'They say after a year or so that the presence is gone. This presence is usually a good feeling that the child is still with them. One mother was even certain that her child's toys had been moved around. But in my experience, bereaved parents on the whole find things like spiritualism unhelpful. They may need to find an answer and sometimes feel the need to experiment. But what they want is to have the child back and to be told he is trying to get in touch, rubs their loss in even more. They are still divided even if there is contact.'

I remembered a story told to me of Sarah, who lost her two-year-old in an accident. She had a recurring dream that she was allowed to take the child out of his grave for an hour every day. She took his pushchair down to the grave to collect him, but could not bear having to take him back to the grave afterwards. This desire to have her son return to her is echoed through the ages by countless mothers. 'The whole point of grieving is to accept and recognise that death is final,' said Tessa. 'Searching is part of eventually accepting that a child is not going to return to his body. Coming to terms with this is a huge thing. The second year is worse than the first. By the second year, a parent can no longer 'pretend' that their child has just gone on a long holiday. The loss of a child is perceived by people in general as an outrage. It is seen as wrong, against the pattern of life, of growing up and the hope that the child will have children of his own some day. Death is not seen as part of life and people are not comfortable around the idea. Death is guaranteed to happen to all of us, but when it happens to a child, it is out of key and even more of a no-go area. Families who have lost a child say that things that were important before, such as buying a new car and or getting a better job become completely irrelevant. Quite a few mothers threaten to commit suicide to try to be with their dead children. But I try to tell them that we have no idea what happens after death and that they may not be with their child. There is terrific stress in having a child ill over a period of time, months or even years, and it can be a great strain especially on the mother coping with the everyday care.

'Brothers and sisters often have a rough time when their sibling is terminally ill. The sick child needs a lot of the attention, so the other children will be used to looking after themselves and getting their own tea. Before a child dies, life for the other children in the family is uncertain to say the least. Plans can never be relied on. Holidays may have to be cancelled because the child is sick again. It is never safe to say what you are going to do. Mum may say she will meet you from school, but the sick child may suddenly get rushed to hospital. Then when the sick child dies, mum suddenly comes back and tries to take over again.

'The death of a child is not something that will go away quickly. Parents do get over it, but only in their own time. One mother, after three and a half years of waking up with stabbing pains, had said that she still felt a sadness but it had become bearable and she admitted 'hat she didn't really want the sadness to go away. Another said on the tenth anniversary of her first child's cot death, "A little bit will always be sad." Parents always need the little bit of sadness there, for the child existed and does not exist any longer.'

Eleven-year-old Garvan Byrne had a very rare form of bone marrow disease. I watched a video in which he talked about what it was like to be dying. He said, 'At first I was very frightened when I knew I was going to die. But I feel much better now. I believe in a life after death. I believe life there will be joyful and happy and there will be no pain. My pain and suffering will be over with. Jesus is a very special friend to me. He always has his arms outstretched to me when I am in trouble. When I die, I will leave my body behind. It is only a reflection, only a tag to say this is Garvan. This is me. When I die, my reflection fades and is left behind. The real self, the inner me, goes up to God.'

15

Where the Magic Goes

Most of the stories I gathered about ghosts and fairies at the bottom of the garden came from older people looking back on their childhood. The response to my inquiries from young people had not been that encouraging and I wondered whether cartoons like *Ghostbusters* had zapped all the magic for today's children. So I decided to visit a local playgroup and infants school. The playgroup children were particularly hard to interview as it involved squatting in Wendy houses, eating grey lumps of pastry and wrestling with pieces of a giant construction set. And the interviewees had a habit of disappearing in mid-sentence and coming back ten minutes later to carry on where they had left off.

Four-year-old Martin had no illusions about ghosts and fairies. 'I've got a Ghostbuster gun, so nothing scares me. Father Christmas is going to bring me a bike. He gets it from the shop of course,' he said looking at me as if I were a bit simple-minded when I mentioned elves.

Polly, wearing a pink ballet dress from the dressing-up box and her friend Nicky, clad in a white dress and crown, both aged four, looked a little more like kindred spirits. 'Fairies are true, aren't they?' I asked hopefully, loading the question in the most unscientific way possible. 'Fairies are just a story,' Polly informed me, pushing a boy out of the way. 'I like Ghostbusters best,' said Nicky. 'There are some scary ghosts and some friendly ghosts. But they're not scary really, 'cos they're on the telly.'

Four-year-old Nicholas joined in while pounding at some pastry. 'I've got a Ghostbuster gun. I shoot witches with it. I see them flying round the house. Monsters don't scare me, though. I put them in a cage with rocks. Monsters are green and red and orange. If I saw them I'd shoot them. His thoughts then turned away from mayhem long enough for him to add: 'I saw fairies in Reading with Father Christmas. I talked to them.' 'They might just be dressed up as fairies,' Nicky threw in scornfully and Nadia, who is three, also added, 'If your teeth are wobbling though, the tooth fairy comes to take them and she makes another one grow and she gives you money, but it hasn't happened to me yet.'

'Where are all the fairies?' I asked Jill, the playgroup leader. 'It's all fighting these days,' she said. 'The boys rush around playing fighting all the time. I say, "Don't make guns," but they just reply, "They're not guns, they're zappers." So I say, "No guns and no zappers please." The girls are more into imaginative games, but it's mainly houses or schools. It's rare to find a boy who's into imaginative games. It's a pity the magic's gone.'

Ann, a mother-helper at the group, blamed the children's cartoons on television for the violence which had replaced imaginative play. 'My son hasn't watched half of *Thundercats* before he's off to find something to hit his sister with. It's our own fault really. We sit the kids in front of the telly or video and don't give them time. But perhaps we haven't got any time to give them anymore.'

It is often felt that left to their own devices, children's imaginations will run riot and that formal education somehow stifles this natural development. But at the local infants school, to which many of the playgroup's children eventually go, the pupils I talked to knew all about witches and magic and dragons, though many had their doubts as to where it all fitted into their daily lives.

Katy, aged five told me: 'I think about witches in my head and then I dream about them. They take me away into the dungeons and they eat me up. Then I wake up and go to mummy and daddy's room. Witches are only pretend though, I think.'

Five-year-old Jamie snuggled up to me and said: 'I don't know if there are ordinary fairies. There's tooth fairies. I've seen them, I think. My big brother is seven. He had three teeth come out when he was six. They came out on different days so the tooth fairy took them away on different nights. I know about magic too. I've got a tape about magic. It's about a magical sword. When you touch it – a miracle! That was when England was true. It happened a long time ago. There is no magic now because all the wizards are dead, though Father Christmas can magic through doors. You can sometimes leave a window open for him, but he might not fit.'

Christopher, also five, said, 'There are real ghosts. They live in a house. But the house is not in this country. This is a safe place to live. You can find dragons in a sort of jungle, but it's stacks of ways from here. Dragons are very, very dangerous. They are more dangerous than witches. They can breathe fire and they can have fire in their tummy. If you got a hose and sprayed water into the dragon's mouth, smoke would come out of his nose.'

Saffron, aged five, told me: 'If I could do magic, I'd turn my goldfish into frogs. I don't like goldfish much. Dragons I like. They breathe fire. They make me laugh, but they're not real.'

Tamesin, aged seven, nearly missed out on the tooth fairy. 'Once I swallowed one of my teeth. I fell over and swallowed it. Damien, my brother, said, "Oh yeah," but I did. So I wrote a letter to the tooth fairy telling her what happened and put it under my pillow and I still got my money.'

John, aged five said: 'My big brother is nine. He got £1 from the tooth fairy. I haven't lost any teeth yet, but one is getting very wobbly,' he added hopefully, giving it a quick tug. 'Dragons were long ago when no one was born. Giants lived thousands of years ago. They used to eat little boys up, but they're all gone now.'

It is debateable whether television feeds children with information or stifles their creative thinking. The views of the children I talked to were heavily influenced by television, but they were also affected by the area in which they lived and their surroundings generally. Put a couple of children in a manor house dating back centuries, surround them with old portraits and push into them the family history dating back generations and it's odds on that they will start seeing ghosts.

Joan Penelope Cope's family had lived in Bramshill House in Berkshire for generations and she claims to have seen dozens of ghosts. Even in her pram she saw 'green man', a creature reputed to appear in the shrubbery. Her childhood was filled with ghosts as she played in the old rooms and the extensive grounds. When she was seven, a ghost came to her room one night. 'I found myself gazing at a youngish woman who must have once been quite good-looking – even a beauty, but death had deprived her of her charms – her eyes were black with a kind of dead light in them.' Her brother saw the ghost too in his room.

It would seem that to be rich or powerful and live in a grand old house does make it more possible to acknowledge ghosts without being called cranky. In more ordinary families, the children often keep their psychic experiences secret from the outside world and sometimes from their parents, which can have all sorts of implications for the family chemistry. Those who do see ghosts, quickly come to learn that it is not acceptable to admit this generally, so they have to hide what is a valid part of their lives or risk being labelled as odd.

However, if a mother also sees ghosts or has supernatural experiences, the child's already receptive mind may pick up the message – 'It's OK to be psychic'. This can be seen as a power ploy by the mother or the child to exclude the father, especially if the mother is lonely and wants to hang on to the child. Also there would seem to be a gender issue as well. Boys tend to grow out of the psychic stage or at least keep it under wraps even from the family, whereas girls can think, 'Mum's psychic so it's okay for me to be psychic when I'm grown up.' So the psychic thing carries on from generation to generation almost ritualistically.

The Cope family's rituals ended with the sale of their grand house and today it belongs to the Home Office and is a training college for high-flying policemen. Despite the blocks of flats which have been built in the wooded grounds and Whitehall's 'improvements' to the property it still retains the magic which influenced the young Miss Cope so deeply. I toured it one evening with my husband and we were regaled with stories of various ghosts said to stalk the stately home, with no respect for the forces of law and order now settled there. As we stood on the grand terrace, staring out across the fields in the twilight, I was shaken to see white forms approaching us, gliding over the ground. 'Ghosts!' I thought immediately. But the figures were not ghosts. They were deer, members of the herd of rare white deer, kept in the house grounds. It was a vivid example of how the power of suggestion can work.

If instead of two well brought-up children with a sense of history like the Cope children, you put a rowdy mob of ghostbusting schoolboys into a stately home, could the magic still work? Not according to my eldest boy, Tom, who went on a school trip to Ufton Court, an Elizabethan manor house in Berkshire, now used by the local education authority. 'We stayed for three days, and you'd have expected there to be loads of ghosts with all that history, but if there were, they kept pretty quiet. We found the priest holes but there were no old priests hiding in them though and we saw some secret passages, but they were covered up by glass and there were still no spooks. But then we didn't really expect any. Most of us think they're a load of rubbish – just like *Ghostbusters* on TV – kid's stuff.

'But not Martin – he believes in anything and he wanted to find a ghost. In the evenings we were allowed to

wander round and he went walking around on his own –
reckoned he'd do better without us. The first night he
drew a blank and by the second night, there still wasn't
even a whiff of a haunting. But on the morning we were
going home, he told us he had seen a peasant with a
muddy face walking around with a brown sort of robe on.
Another boy said "Oh, yes, I bet." Then when we got back
to school, Martin said, "You know that ghost, I didn't
really see it. I just said I did for a joke." So there weren't
any ghosts after all at Ufton Court. I never thought there
were. If there had been, I expect they'd have been too
busy watching *Neighbours* to bother with us.'

Would it have been different for Tom and his hard-
headed friends if they had gone singly to a supposedly
haunted house instead of in a rowdy group. James is quite
a practical sensible lad but at an old house in the Cot-
swolds, things went bump in the night for him. 'We found
a room that was pink,' he told me 'and the first night my
mum tried to sleep in it but moved out in the middle of
the night into a different room. The next night my dog
slept in the room and also moved out in the middle of the
night. So the next night I slept in the room with the dog
on the floor and me and the dog could sense that something was there, because the dog started to growl for no
reason and started whining and ran out. Then I went back
to sleep, but I could feel there was someone there. The
room started shaking and I could hear voices, dim ones.
Then my back went cold and I screamed and ran out. The
next morning I told my mum what had happened and she
said that perhaps someone had died in the room and
come back for their soul.'

Sometimes the magic of a place can survive despite the

crowds. Polly and her ten-year-old daughter, Sarah, reacted strongly against the stone circles of Avebury, just
like Emma and her mother who I mentioned in Chapter
9, though in this case there was no underlying stress in
the family. They got to Avebury and refused point blank
to go in. Polly told me: 'There were no birds and I got a
nasty feeling. Sarah grabbed my hand and wouldn't even
cross the road.' At the time there was a very creepy children's series on television that was set at Avebury Rings,
which was why Polly and Sarah went to see them. Afterwards, Sarah refused to watch the series. Perhaps it was a
case of things going full circle and television, the alleged
imagination killer, helping to bolster the old mythology.
But Polly says she got the same feeling at Stonehenge and
at Loch Ness. 'Again there were no birds,' she said.

There may be places, that because of things that happened there to people long ago, that do give off bad vibrations, to which children especially may be sensitive. If so
it failed to work for the Eason family when we visited Avebury Rings. The children knew it was a magic place and
that, in the interests of research, I was determined to
touch every one of the stones. The older children were
reasonably obliging at first, but after about a quarter of
an hour, eight-year-old Jade started to complain.
'There's nothing happening. It's not magic. Can't we go
somewhere more interesting?' she said and went to sulk
in the shade of the largest stone. Jack, as usual when
called upon to perform, showed no sign of any psychic
ability but wandered off in search of what he said was a
seal in a lake but which looked suspiciously like a stone in
a far field. Sixteen-month-old Bill just wanted to escape,
preferably onto the main road which looked suitably

dangerous and Miranda began a whine for an ice cream. Her whining could have been put down to bad vibrations but for the fact that she does this on most outings. I got quite excited when I felt one stone actually vibrating under my hand but as Tom pointed out, Jack had returned from his unsuccessful seal hunt and was round the other side of the stone kicking it.

While we may have got no response from an ancient monument, on the other side of the world, Ally and her family felt something at a 'new ancient monument'. Ally, who lives in North Carolina, wrote to tell me that while her family were travelling through British Columbia in Canada in the spring of 1989, they came across a hotel where the proprietor had put together a 'ghost' town from a collection of old buildings brought from elsewhere. 'Included was a wonderfully restored saloon which we visited. The rest of the family had gone down the outside steps and was beginning to walk along the road when there was an agonised cry from Timothy, my four-year-old son, who was stumbling down the steps, clutching the back of his head and screaming that someone was trying to break his head. He described the pain as like a knife. I immediately thought of brain tumours, but neither before nor since has he ever complained of headache or pain. The situation we were in and the terror he exhibited for those few minutes convince me that he was in fact involved in an incident from the past.'

This might not be evidence enough to convince other people, but as I have tried to show in this book the moments when our world brushes against the psychic world are fleeting. Afterwards people can only say: 'Well this happened to me and it has changed my life in this way and I can find no other explanation for it.' And as I have also pointed out, for some children this brush with the beyond may be no big deal at all but just another part of a life which is already confusing enough, because of the number of things children have to confront for the first time. Also, for some children, a psychic experience can only be faced and interpreted in later life. As Ivy said in Chapter 9, looking back on the goblin-like creatures who terrorised her when she was young, it is only now that she believes they were not products of her imagination.

We do not know how many children see – for want of better words – ghosts, angels or goblins or what proportion of these are fantasy or psychic phenomena. Neither can we be sure, when a child has seen something from another world, if he or she is describing it correctly or in terms that come closest to his or her limited experience. As I have related, Jack once told me that he had seen an 'enormous panda bear' in the New Forest which turned out to be a large black and white cow. A child who does see some sort of shining messenger from heaven may well translate this in terms of the tinsel-winged angels he or she has been taught to expect.

Though some psychologists and psychiatrists are very nervous about it, the psychic world of the normal child has much to teach them about family stress and the child's way of coping with it. Parents also need to learn to cope with a child's contact with the paranormal. Children can be damaged if their experiences are ridiculed or dismissed. Every experience and fear has to be discussed in a caring and open-minded way. Even if the experience is patently not paranormal, it is real to the child and could be affecting his or her sense of well-being. If it is psychic, then it casts a new insight onto our mundane world.

Should psychic powers be encouraged? This is a tricky question, especially when it is difficult enough to cultivate the normal abilities a child possesses. We do not know the extent of the psychic world and in attempting to do more than appreciate those rare glimpses we get of it, we could distort it or give it a place in children's lives where they feel either obliged to perform or are afraid of what would seem to be a natural ability, that sometimes fades or lies dormant until the child's own offspring re-open the door. Perhaps all we can do is give the child time and space and a caring and supportive environment.

Today there are many commercial pressures which bear down on the spiritual lives of our children (in the fullest sense of spiritual, which embraces more than the psychic world or churchgoing). Proper values often take second place to a shiny new bike and the latest video games. Perhaps we should deal with these before trying to tackle new frontiers. Furthermore, do you want your child to be able to monitor your every thought or, worse still, as telepathy is a two-way process to have their incessant chatter running ceaselessly through your mind? And supposing you had a premonition every time your child was going to fall over in the playground or get bopped by one of his friends? What would you do? You could hardly write a note to school saying – 'Please excuse my child from play this week as he might fall off the climbing frame at a quarter to one next Thursday!'

Worst of all, supposing your children could take off in their astral bodies? It's hard enough getting the real body to bed without having an astral form popping back down to watch the late night film with you. It would play havoc with discipline and that last resort – 'Get to your room and stay there (before I get out the axe)' – would be meaningless. The physical body might obey but five minutes later the astral form would be whizzing round the living room.